BUFF

by Robert Ackerman

DORRANCE PUBLISHING CO
EST. 1920
PITTSBURGH, PENNSYLVANIA 15238

Dorrance Publishing Co
585 Alpha Drive
Suite 103
Pittsburgh, PA 15238
Visit our website at *www.dorrancebookstore.com*

ISBN: 979-8-8892-5465-2
eISBN: 979-8-8892-5965-7

Vera Means was a full-blooded Lakota Sioux. She was beautiful and was six foot and one inch tall. She carried herself with a regal bearing and she was pregnant. Her husband, Dawson Means, was of Irish descent. He worked about 40 miles away from the main city hospital fixing methane gas leaks on old natural gas and oil lines.

Dawson and Vera owned a 1,000-acre buffalo ranch and they were well off. He didn't like the feeling he got when they shipped his Buffalo for slaughter. The Buffalo were the second most sacred animal in the Lakota religion, next to the Eagle.

Vera's water broke about a week early and they rushed her to the operating room for a C-Section. Her doctor had known for months that she was going to have to have a C-Section because she was carrying a very large baby. They didn't know it would be the largest baby they would ever see. The hospital was buzzing as the staff spoke of the huge, huge baby that would arrive soon.

Dawson got a call from Regional Hospital and they told him that his wife was soon going into the operating room. Dawson threw his tools in the back of his truck and sped to the hospital. He turned a 40-minute drive into a 30-minute one and rushed into the emergency room. He was quickly escorted to a waiting room. Soon a short, fat doctor with dark hair came in and introduced himself as Dr. Warson.

"Congratulations! You're the proud father of the biggest baby ever born at Regional Hospital. Your son weighs 17 pounds and 8 ounces. I have to tell you that your son has Myostatin-related Muscular hypertrophy," Dr. Warson said.

"Oh no…" Dawson said.

"Don't worry," the doctor answered, "most American men would love to have Myostatin related muscular hypertrophy. He will have perfect health, and he will have huge musculature. If he works out with weights regularly, he could be one of the strongest men in the world. Even if he doesn't work out, he'll be twice as strong as the average person his age."

The infant had brownish/black hair, brown eyes, and a light skin color. Dawson went to see his wife in the recovery room.

"Well, you said you wanted a big boy and you sure got one. What should we name him?" Vera asked.

Dawson answered, "Let's call him Buff because he is certainly going to be Buff, and it will remind us of the sacred buffalo."

"That's a perfect name!" Vera agreed.

Dawson thought about how he couldn't get his head wrapped around the fact that Buff was twice the size of an average baby. He gave Vera a passionate kiss.

Vera was the granddaughter of Sitting Bull and she was admired by the entire tribe. She did volunteer work all over the Pine Ridge Reservation. She often helped the medicine man set up sweat lodges.

Buff's parents planned for there to be a large open house and a Pow-wow when Buff was three months old. Everybody wanted to see the baby. Dawson was welcomed by all. He participated in scores of sweat lodges, several sun dances, vision quests and many Yuwipies.

For the vision quest, the medicine man, Charles placed Dawson on top of Bear Butte with no blanket, no water, and no food. He had nothing but himself. He had a vision after three days and went with the medicine man for an interpretation. He told the medicine man that he saw Buff working as a lawman who carried a huge handgun. The medicine man said, "This is an easy one. Your son is going to be a lawman. I suspect he will eventually be Sheriff of Pennington County."

Dawson asked if he would do a special healing sweat to try to cure his terrible psoriasis. His shins were open sores from where Dawson kept peeling the scales off.

Charles, the medicine man, organized the sweat. There were 7 people in the sweat. Including Dawson and the medicine man, Charles.

During the first door, opening the flap, they all prayed and sang to a drum beat. Everybody always prayed for their family's health and longevity first.

During the second door, the fireman added 9 more red, glowing lava rocks in the pit in the middle of the lodge. After they closed the flap, Charles, the medicine man, called in two spirits. He asked everyone to pray for the curing of Dawson's psoriasis.

The spirits were blue orbs with gold fringes and each was about the size of a beach ball.

During the third door, the fireman brought in 9 more rocks. The orbs were balls of pulsating energy. Charles sang some prayers for Dawson's healing. He then rubbed bear grease vigorously onto Dawson's psoriasis. Within three weeks Dawson's psoriasis was completely cured.

Dawson had turned his garage into a workout room with dumbbells, a gymnastic ring, a bench press, and free weights. He put a large punching bag in the corner. He bought a recumbent bike and machines for all muscle groups.

Dawson started Buff lifting weights at three years old. At three years old, Buff could do the cross on the gymnastic rings. Dawson worked out for three hours every morning and Buff was always with him.

When Buff turned 12 years old, Dawson took Buff to his job with him. Buff was 6 foot 2 inches tall and weighed 210 pounds. Dawson showed him how he was fixing methane leaks.

The first day that Dawson took Buff to his job with him, Buff took off and started exploring an old, abandoned gold mine that was about 150 yards from where his dad was.

Dawson's boss hadn't checked up on him for three years, besides the weekly phone calls. He wasn't worried about getting in trouble.

What he didn't know was that his supervisor, Gordon Thatcher, was filming him from a spot about 100 yards away. Gordon checked and recorded all his employees periodically with his massive lens. He had never been caught by any of his employees.

Dawson finished tightening the very large bolts after he put in a new gasket. He then checked the methane meter and saw the leak was fixed. Two four-door pickup trucks pulled up next to Dawson and six men got out with four-foot-long heavy pipes. The driver of the truck said to Dawson, "You beat up our good friend, Butch Skillman. We're gonna give you some of your own medicine."

"He attacked me and I defended myself. He just wouldn't give up so I knocked him out," Dawson explained.

"You beat the shit out of him! Butch was in the hospital for a week. You broke his jaw," the man said menacingly and swung his pipe at Dawson's head. Dawson jumped back; so the pipe missed his head. He jumped forward again and struck the guy with a straight right hand to the big guy's nose, flattening it. The man dropped to the ground, out cold.

All five of the other men rushed Dawson and pummeled him with their pipes.

Buff heard what was happening, and he sprinted 150 yards to help his dad. The twelve year old grabbed one guy and threw him about six feet.

Another roughneck with a pipe had gotten behind Buff and struck him in the back of his head. Buff fell on his face, unconscious.

Dawson was struck with a pipe in the forehead. He was out cold too. The men kicked and beat Dawson and Buff mercilessly. They knocked out seven of Dawson's front teeth. The men pounded on Dawson and Buff for five more minutes. They beat on their victim's back, legs, buttocks, and even their feet. Then they turned the unconscious men over and beat them viciously some more.

An hour later, Dawson woke up and realized he was paralyzed from the waist down. Buff was still out cold. Dawson called for two evac helicopters from Regional Hospital. The choppers arrived about 20 minutes later. They quickly loaded the men on backboards after they put neck braces on them.

Buff woke up five hours later in pain all over his body. He heard a voice that said, "Someday you'll heal with your hands." Buff realized it was God speaking to him.

His nurse told him that he had a concussion, and they would wake him up every two hours all night to check on him. He was black and blue all over his body and he knew the bruises would just get darker over the next day or two. The nurse pushed four milligrams of morphine into his IV line. She promised to give him morphine as needed. "Just push this red button and I'll be here," said the nurse.

Dawson was bleeding internally from his liver and one kidney. They had to do emergency surgery. They put him in the ICU for two days after his surgery. He was then transferred to a regular room. He had a brace on his lumbar spine. Luckily his spinal cord was not completely cut.

Vera stayed at the hospital comforting her men for four days for Buff and seven days for Dawson, but she did take a quick shower every day.

On Dawson's third day, Gordon Thatcher, his boss, came to visit him. He was a tall thin man with gray hair and he wore camo-colored clothing. Grayson said, "I'm so sorry about your back and the beating you took. I was filming you from about 100 yards away. I occasionally video all of my workers that way. I was videoing when they beat the shit out of you and Buff. I was too far away to have run to help you. Look at me Dawson, I only weigh 140 pounds. The good news is that I took the video to the sheriff and the chief of police. As soon as they watched it, they rounded up the six roughnecks. They charged them all with attempted murder. With the video evidence, they all knew there was no way out; so they all confessed. Soon, they will be spending 10-20 years in prison."

After six months had passed, Dawson got a check from the company for 2.4 million dollars. He sold his buffalo ranch too, but he kept his huge log home. He got 4.78 million dollars for his 1,000 acres of prime grassland and 1,500 buffalo. He gave 2 million dollars to the Pine Ridge Reservation, the poorest county in the United States.

Dawson wasn't the type to feel sorry for himself. He called in his contractor friend, John Lintz, and asked him if he could do some work for him.

"I'm so sorry about your back," John said.

"Well, at least I have my upper body," Dawson said.

"What can I do for you, Dawson?" John asked. "Can you build me a wheelchair ramp to the front door?"

"Of course," John answered. "I also want an addition to the garage, something about the size of a five car garage with a garage door. I ordered tons of workout equipment for Buff and me."

Later, Dawson asked Buff, "Would you take the Krav Maga class to go along with your karate class?"

"Great Dad," Buff said. "I love martial arts. I'm going to start a workout time for weight lifting with free weights and the machines. I'm going to work out and run six miles a day from now on."

Dawson had seven teeth implanted. He felt so much better with his big white smile. He started working out again along with Buff in his new gym addition.

Buff was going to make sure that what happened to his dad and him would never happen again.

Doug was Buff's Sensei for taekwondo. It is probably the best kicking martial art. Sensei Doug said to Dawson, "I've never worked with such a strong, coordinated, and fast young man. I've also started teaching him kickboxing."

Buff had 19-inch biceps by the time he reached 14 years old. He eventually would have 24-inch biceps.

By the time Buff was 14 he was already a black belt in karate, and by the time he was 16, he had a 2nd-degree black belt.

Dawson had made special arrangements for Buff with his karate sensei, Ito. They decided every Saturday morning they would have a two-hour session for $200. This gave Buff time to go to all his Krav Maga and other martial arts classes.

Sensei Ito was an eighth-degree black belt from Okinawa, Japan. He moved to Rapid City when his sister moved to Rapid City. She married a Colonel who was then stationed at Ellsworth, AFB. Ito grew to love Rapid City.

Buff graduated from high school at 16 years old because they moved him up two grades when he was 13 years old. He had an IQ of 140.

Buff worked out like a man possessed. He wanted to get huge and to be able to take on six guys to win a fight like he experienced with his dad. Some days, he worked out for eight hours. He spent a while stretching and doing a few yoga poses that he had learned from his mother. Mostly Buff practiced his martial arts moves.

Sensei David was a tall muscular man from Israel and he had been an officer in the Israeli military. The Israeli army trained their troops in the use of Krav Maga and David was the best. He had started a Krav Maga Dojo as a third-degree black belt. He was vacationing in the Black Hills and thought Rapid City was the most perfect little city he'd ever been to; so he moved here.

Sensei David asked Dawson to come to his office. Dawson never missed one of Buff's training sessions and he was making many new friends. David said, "Buff can hit harder, faster, and stronger than my friend, Frank, who has a fifth-degree black belt."

"No one wants to get in the ring with him. I'm trying to get him to let off on his strikes, but it is hard for Buff to let off because in all his martial arts they taught people to strike an opponent through the target. David bought special pads for Buff's hands and thick pads for his feet so he could get in the ring with Buff. More and more often David found himself on the mat. Krav Maga was the only martial art that had no rules."

Doug, Buff's Taekwondo sensei, called Dawson over to a quiet corner of the Dojo. Doug said, "Buff is progressing so fast that he is already the toughest man in the dojo." Doug asked Dawson if he could continue to teach Buff Kickboxing.

Dawson had a gun range on the old buffalo ranch that he had sold. The new owners said they could use it anytime. When Buff was 10 years old, his dad first took him to the gun range. Very quickly Buff graduated from a 16 gauge shotgun to a twelve gauge. His dad moved him from a 22 rifle to an AR-15.

There was a skeet and trap section on the firing range. They shot skeet and trap often. Buff and Dawson shot at targets at a hundred yards, two hundred yards, and three hundred yards. Dawson also got Buff a Glock pistol. He shot six days a week until he was an expert marksman.

When Buff was a few weeks from turning 17 years old, he asked his dad if it would be okay for him to become a Marine. Dawson said, "I'd be proud for you to become a Marine."

On his 17th Birthday, Buff and his dad went to the Marine Corps recruiter's office. Tech Sergeant Quaal said, "I can't believe you are only seventeen. Let's get you measured."

The recruiters measured Buff's height at 6' 8". He weighed in at 275 pounds of muscle with a 33-inch waist. They asked him if he could do 100 push-ups. Buff did them in under 100 seconds. They were blown away because almost none of the recruits could do 100 pushups with perfect form.

Tech Sergeant Quaal said, "Well, I see you're in perfect shape, now you have to pass the intelligence test."

Buff finished the test and they took it to the desk in the back of the room to grade it. After a few minutes, Quaal said, "You have one of the highest scores we've ever had. What would you like to do in the Marines?"

"I want to be a military policeman," Buff answered enthusiastically.

"I promise you, I'll try to pull some strings to get you into the military police when you graduate."

"When does the next boot camp start?" Buff asked.

"The next one starts in two weeks," Quaal said.

"I'll be ready in two weeks!" Buff answered.

When Dawson and Buff got home they went to tell Vera. She was proud, but a little scared about Buff joining the Marines.

"Next week we'll have a pow-wow for you. You and some friends can do a sweat just before the pow-wow starts," Vera offered.

The next week they had a large pow-wow. There was every kind of dancer there. There were fancy, grass, and shawl dancers. There were also prairie chicken and traditional dancers. Two-thirds of the crowd was Lakota.

They had Buff sit in the middle of the circle.

After the pow-wow, there were cheers all around.

"Thank you all for coming and bringing food!" Vera yelled. She was still wearing her traditional dancing costume and looked radiant. She had a perfectly shaped, tall body and she was arguably the best-looking woman there. Her black hair was very long and shiny.

"Now, let's have a feast," Vera announced. The crowd cheered.

Later that night, Dawson told Vera, "I love you so much. You were the most beautiful woman at the pow-wow."

"Well, you were the most beautiful man I've ever seen," she said.

"Please don't call me 'beautiful,' honey," Dawson complained and they both broke out laughing. Dawson stopped smiling and got serious.

He said, "Vera, can we make love tonight?"

"I thought you'd never ask."

Dawson made sure Vera climaxed and then Vera stimulated Dawson until he came. Since his spinal cord wasn't completely cut, Vera learned how to pleasure him by putting a constriction band on his penis.

Eight days later, Buff reached the recruit training center at Parris Island. They first had all the recruits stand at attention on yellow footprints. The drill sergeants split them up into troops of 43 Marines to be trained by one drill sergeant each.

The first thing they did at boot camp was to buzz cut all the recruits' hair. Dawson thought of the Native boys at boarding school on the reservation who had their long hair cut off by law. Back then, the government's motto was, "Kill the Indian and save the man." The boys' long hair had given them a sense of pride.

When Buff went to get his uniform, the sergeant said, "Here's a t-shirt. We didn't have any uniform shirts that fit a 50-inch chest and 22-inch neck. We hired a seamstress who will see you tomorrow for measurements to make you a custom uniform that fits." He handed Buff a pair of pants, a pith helmet, a custom shaving kit, underwear, and boots.

The next day Buff went to see the seamstress and his uniform shirts were ready.

On the first training day, they ran a timed 2.5 miles. It was an easy run for Buff, but he saw most of the troops were struggling. They then had to do 50 pushups, 50 sit-ups, and 10 pull-ups. Those that couldn't do that many were put in an upper body strength program.

The next few days, they learned to march. They marched everywhere. They learned fast that they better follow orders. If they were to do something, they'd better do it quickly and right, and treat their drill sergeant with the utmost respect.

In Phase II - Weeks 5-9 they practiced rifle and pistol marksmanship training, field training, rifle training, gas chamber training, the field firing range, and finally the 'Crucible.'

Buff had a ball shooting at targets 200, 300, and 500 yards away. Buff was the only one that didn't miss any shots. They had to run through a field of pop-up targets and Buff only missed one. He was now an expert marksman. He had a combined score of 350. He was only the second man on Paris Island to reach that score.

They then shot with pistols. Buff again reached the expert level. Buff scored 375, which he was proud of because he hadn't practiced with a pistol as much as the rifle.

In Phase III, everybody had to qualify for swimming. Buff had grown up swimming in stock dams and the Missouri River all through his childhood. He passed the swimming test easily. Then he had a defensive driving course test. He barely passed it because he had mostly only driven on country dirt roads.

Then came the teaching of Marine Corps history, first aid, more physical training drills, and inspection before they moved on to the confidence course. It was an eleven station obstacle course that was supposed to help build the troop's confidence as well as their upper body strength. Recruits had to tackle the course twice during the thirteen weeks of training. Four of the guys dropped out because it was too much for them.

The three-day field training introduced the troops to field living conditions. During the event, they learned basic field skills in how to set up a tent, how to build a field sanitation area, how to use camouflage, and they had to go through the gas room again.

The field firing range was an application of training devoted to firing weapons in field conditions. They also learned to fire at moving targets under low light conditions while wearing gas masks.

Then came the Crucible. It emphasized trainee teamwork under stress. Recruits get 8 hours of sleep during the entire 54-hour course. They had to ration food themselves. Each received two and a half meals or MREs to eat over the 54-hour course. Then they were put through long road marches and a night infiltration course. They marched 54 miles in those 54 days.

The Crucible started at three in the morning with a six-mile fast march. The obstacle course was brutal, and Buff was never so happy when he finished it the second time. He had never been so exhausted in his life. The drill sergeant led them on a road march from their barracks to the training field which was 8 miles away. They placed their gear in huts and prepared for the first of four, four-hour events. Each event had several warrior stations that each team had to work together to solve.

One warrior station was built around an enemy-mined rope bridge that the recruits must cross with their gear and ammunition boxes. They were only given a couple of short pieces of rope.

"Anyone know how to defuse a mine?" the drill sergeant asked.

A tall recruit standing next to Buff said, "I think if we just step on them, that should do it."

"Very funny," said the drill sergeant.

Buff offered, "I think I figured out what to do. Those mines need someone to step on them for them to explode. Let's use these two small lengths of rope to move the mines after we make room to get the ropes around them."

They all had folding shovels so they dug around the mines, making sloped edges so they could wrap the ropes securely around the mines.

"Well, I'm not going to do it!" a nearby recruit whined.

Buff made a lasso and placed it around the middle of the mine. Then he pulled the mine out of the hole to the side of the road. He did the same with the second mine.

At another event, the troops were divided in half and teams battled each other with pugil sticks. Buff knocked his opponents down like dominos.

After the event, they had to do a five-mile run, then they got four hours of sleep, and then finished the final two events.

At the end of the second day, the troops went through a night infiltration again. They got four more hours of sleep. When they were told to get their lazy asses out of bed, they force-marched nine miles to the end of the Crucible.

Buff had never marched for 54 miles in 54 hours. He had blisters all over his feet as did most of the others. But they did it! Buff graduated, and now he was a United States Marine.

The next step was to get specialized training in whatever job each Marine was picked for. Buff was convinced that being a military Policeman would be the best use of his skills. They often turned very big men into Marine policemen; so it didn't take too much convincing for Buff's superiors to send him to military police training.

He was sent to military Police school at the Marine Corps detachment at Fort Leonard Wood, Missouri. It was a 20-week course to learn various law enforcement techniques using a combination of verbal instruction and practical applications. They had hands-on instruction in firearms, non-lethal weapons and techniques, law enforcement subjects, use of force, force protection, and basic reaction force continuum.

In the dorm one night, eight guys decided to give Buff a blanket party.

His good friend, Rick, slept next to his bunk. Eight guys surrounded Buff and started to pummel him. Rick tried to help Buff. Buff was out of his bed like a shot. He palm heel struck one guy in the nose and knocked him out. He kicked another one in the balls and he went down. He head-butted another one and he was knocked out cold. He straight punched the last guy on the side of the bed where he was fighting.

He was out like a light.

Buff rushed to the other side of the bed to roundhouse-kick one of the guys in the head. He went down. Then he threw an elbow strike to another guy's head and he went down. Rick knocked one guy out, and Buff finished off the last guy with a jump kick to the face. He was out.

"Thanks, Rick," Buff said.

"Well, you did most of the work," Rick answered. Nobody bothered Buff or Rick again.

They learned more about cleaning and handling their weapons, defensive driving tactics, penal codes, military law, and security protection tactics. Two weeks before graduation, the Afghanistan war started, on October 7th, 2001.

After Buff and the rest of the troops graduated they started sending military police to Afghanistan because of the Marines' special training and the lack of manpower.

When Buff got there he was assigned a Humvee with a mounted 60-caliber machine gun.

He would be sent on many patrols with another recruit, who had a Belgian Malinois. His troops would also go to small towns to talk to the elders with an interpreter. They tried to get the elderly Afghanis to trust and help them. Many did help. Some were instantly a lifeline to the Taliban.

Buff also had been issued an M-4 rifle, so he could launch grenades with it. The M-4 has 30 round magazines, and Buff carried ten magazines in his pockets. He bought a large knife with a sheath at the military store and he strapped it to his left ankle. They let the huge man continue to carry a 44 magnum on his belt, due to its stopping power and Buff's strength.

Buff armed himself with a quick-release bulletproof vest, and integrated breathing and floatation device as well as load-bearing equipment.

He missed his three best friends from school. They met for dinner every Saturday night. His friends and he were mostly of like minds. One of his friends, Dave, told Buff a story of his enlightenment a couple of years before. David had been hospitalized for days with pneumonia. On the fourth day, he had on his civilian clothes and was standing in front of the nurse's station waiting to be discharged.

While he was waiting, suddenly, there was a still, small voice in his head, speaking to him. It said, "13.8 billion years ago God was a singularity of infinite density, infinite gravity, and infinite intelligence."

The voice asked, "How can they call my creation 'the big bang?' … There were no ears to hear it. Let's call it the great expansion from which I created everything needed to form the galaxies, stars, planets - including your earth."

Buff loved the story and believed it to be true. He believed in God and Dave's story and it gave him comfort.

Buff's first mission in Afghanistan was to go with eight other Marines to an adobe building about 12 clicks (kilometers) away from camp.

One of the leaders of the Taliban, was said to be staying there and they wanted him dead or alive. The marines took their four Humvees about 250 yards from the Taliban's house that was just over a small hill.

The Marines surrounded the building and yelled for the leader to come out with his hands up. Automatic gunfire came from all four of the windows on the west side of the house.

Buff decided to carry his M-60 machine gun that had been mounted on his Humvee and strapped his M-4 rifle over his shoulder. He had four rocket-propelled grenades with him. He was big and strong enough to easily shoot the 60 caliber accurately from a standing position. He opened up on the building's windows and sides and took out several fighters. He put down the 60-caliber and grabbed his M-4 and installed the grenade launcher.

He shot a grenade into all four of the windows. The other Marines were pouring fire at the building. Soon the Marines entered the building and found all the Taliban dead. They loaded the leader's body in a Humvee after taking pictures of him. They had taken no casualties and considered the raid a great success.

Two days later, Buff and 10 other Marines traveled two clicks to a tiny town where many elders lived. They hoped to gain their trust and turn them into informants. After getting permission, Buff called the Air Force and asked them if they could have two, A-10 Warthogs fly in circles a couple of miles away. Buff could just smell a trap.

The A-10 thunderbird, often called the Warthog, is basically a flying 30 mm gun. It is a tremendously powerful cannon able to fire at the rate of roughly 4,000 rounds per minute.

As they drove up to about 100 yards away from the town, they saw some of the elders smoking black tar opium in the shade of an adobe house. They stood in a welcoming posture.

The vehicles slowly started approaching, and suddenly at least 100 Taliban came running out of a gully where they had been hidden in small bunkers. They opened up on the Marines and killed three of them instantly. Buff opened up on the Taliban with the 60-caliber machine gun.

The Taliban started dropping like flies, but they kept coming. Buff got on his radio and called the A-10 Warthogs in. He told them to level the west half of the town. In 30 seconds that seemed like forever to the Marines, the first Warthog fired a pair of sidewinder missiles close to the gully and dozens of Taliban went down.

The second Warthog opened up in bursts and blew big holes through the foot-thick adobe walls. They targeted the retreating Taliban and the Warthog took out the remaining Taliban.

They loaded the three dead Marines into the Humvees and they returned to camp. It was a sad night at Camp Leatherneck.

A few days later they went out on another peace mission to a tiny village to try and talk more elders into helping them.

The elders were friendly and told the Marines they were on America's side and the Taliban were evil. The Marines returned to camp in a good mood.

The next couple of visits to villages that were fairly close went well but the Marines knew that Kandahar Province had the most Taliban in Afghanistan. A new mission began. Ten Marines drove to a small village that was fairly far from their base. The farthest they'd ever been so far.

Buff and the nine others drove up to the first building, jumped out and leaned their backs

against the wall. Buff took a quick look inside the building and saw that it was empty. Still, he felt the little hairs on his neck raise up.

They moved forward and took a peek around another corner. A bullet slammed into the wall, just inches from Buff's face. A piece of adobe flew off and it cut a large groove in Buff's right cheek.

Buff just let it bleed because he couldn't put pressure against it right then. He was too busy shooting. Copious amounts of blood flowed down Buff's cheek onto his uniform. He and the rest of the Marines cleared the rest of the town; so they went back to their vehicles. A fellow Marine put a pressure bandage on Buff's cheek and held it tightly there until they reached Camp Leatherneck.

Buff was taken to the infirmary. The doctor looked at the wound and said, "It's so deep, we're going to have to put some sutures down in the wound and then I'll stitch up the outside. Come back if any stitches come out before ten days. The stitches on the inside will dissolve on their own. Come back and I'll take them out, or you can take them out yourself. Just clip the stitch and pull it out away from the knot."

Buff pulled them out after a week and he had a large scar on his cheekbone that he was sure wouldn't fade much. He thought about all the questions he'd get when he got back to the states.

Buff re-upped for another year in Afghanistan. In March 2002, Anaconda was launched with 1,000 Al Qaeda and Taliban fighters in the Shah-i-Kot Valley, south of the city of Gardez, Paktia Province.

Nearly 1,000 U.S. and 1,000 Afghan troops battled. Just as things were wrapping up, Buff got a through-and-through shot to his thigh.

The exit wound was huge. They sent him to Japan for surgery. "The bullet has nicked an artery," said the doctor. "He is very lucky to be alive."

When he had healed up, they didn't send him back to Afghanistan, but they sent him to Parris Island for the remainder of his four years of duty in the Marines.

Buff weighed 275 pounds and had 22" biceps. He reached 6'11" in height. They had Buff start a special program to help get those who were overweight or had weak upper body strength to lose weight and become much stronger. Within just 4 weeks they all could do 10 proper pull-ups and 50 push-ups.

One day while helping the people in his program, he looked back at his past. At age eight, he could deadlift 240 pounds. At ten he could deadlift 285 pounds. When he was 12 he could lift 330 pounds. At the age of 14, he lifted 380 pounds. At 16 he could lift 623.9 pounds. At 17 he could deadlift 1,004 pounds which was only a little over a hundred pounds less than the world record. His bench press was 440.7 pounds, which was almost a world record too.

Buff knew that if he wanted to, he probably could have beaten or come close to beating all the world records. In every spare second, he lifted weights or practiced his martial arts.

Buff had returned to his dad's huge log house after his four years of active duty. His dad had added a couple of leg machines while he was gone. Buff worked out as a man possessed.

He had a body fat level of 6%. His waist was 33 inches. Buff could eat like a horse, and his weight increased to 360 pounds of muscle.

Buff went to see the Pennington County Sheriff, Keith Carlyle. He asked him if he could become a deputy. He showed the sheriff his Marine records and told him about his martial arts training. After the sheriff had gone through his records and saw the dozen or so medals, he sat back in his chair and put his hands behind his head before speaking.

"Hell, yes! You got a job. You'll have to go to Pierre to take four weeks of learning civilian law and tactics. You need to be in Pierre's Law Enforcement Center by Monday."

"Thank you, sir!" Buff replied. The sheriff and Buff shook hands. Buff had seldom been so happy in his life.

When Buff got back from Pierre, Sheriff Carlyle partnered Buff with Deputy Sheriff Sandy Angel. She had blue eyes, blonde hair was 5 '6", and had a first-degree black belt in Krav Maga. She was also gorgeous. Soon, they were the best of friends. Sandy was so lovely that Buff had to make an effort to repress any sexual feelings he had for her. They worked very well together. They quickly busted a big drug operation and collared a pedophile.

While on patrol, Buff and Sandy were called to go to the 7th Avenue Bar. They were told some bikers were tormenting and hitting four Mexicans. Buff and Sandy figured the bikers were armed.

As they walked into the bar and scoped out the scene, they saw eight bikers who had the four Mexicans pinned in a corner and were severely beating them.

"Leave those men alone, you're all under arrest," Buff called out.

The huge leader of the bikers weighed in at about 350 pounds, Buff figured. He had a beer belly but you could tell he pumped iron regularly.

The huge biker charged Buff. Buff hit him in the solar plexus with a jumping front kick. The huge man dropped and lay there trying to get his breath back. The seven remaining bikers charged Buff and Sandy. Sandy hit one of the bikers punching him with a palm heel strike to the man's face. His nose was almost completely flat. The man fell over on his back, completely unconscious. Buff hit one of the charging bikers with a jumping spinning roundhouse kick. It was lights out for him. He then kicked another biker in the balls with all the force he could muster. The man screamed and went to the floor, curled up in a ball.

Buff called for backup and told them they'd need a paddy wagon to transport the eight bikers. Buff and Sandy zip-tied the bikers with their hands behind their backs. The paddy wagon showed up and the police officer, with Buff and Sandy's help, chained them to the floor and put them in real handcuffs. All of them would be charged with assault and battery at the least.

Off duty, Buff and Sandy were driving around town in Buff's SUV when Sheriff Carlyle called them on Buff's mobile phone because didn't want it to go out over the radio. Carlyle said that the Pine Ridge Reservation Police Chief asked if Buff and Sandy could come to the reservation as soon as possible.

"Of course, we can head that way now," Buff said, "What's up?"

"They have two missing girls," Carlyle said.

Almost everybody on the reservation knew Buff and held him in the highest regard. They normally didn't want any outside law enforcement people on the reservation. They had their own. They wanted to take care of their own law enforcement but asking for Buff's help was the exception.

Buff and Sandy stopped by the department and got in their patrol car. They sped to the reservation with lights and sirens heading to the girls' parents' homes first.

The Bernards were waiting out front for them. Mrs. Bernard said that their daughter, Pam, and her friend, Susan White Owl went for a walk the day before and hadn't been seen since.

"Did she have any enemies?" Sandy asked.

Both parents said, "NO."

"She is loved by everyone. She's just the sweetest girl you could ever know." Sandy asked if Susan was a good friend of the others.

"Yes," said the mother.

"Our daughter was best friends with her. Our daughter was close friends with the other four missing girls," Mr. Bernard said.

"They were as thick as thieves. Whoops, I didn't mean..." Mrs. Bernard began.

Sandy stopped her by saying, "You didn't say anything wrong."

Next, Buff and Sandy went to see Susan White Owl's parents. The home they were living in was falling apart. It didn't surprise Buff and Sandy because Pine Ridge was the poorest county in the entire United States. They soon learned that three families shared a small house. They were invited in by Mr. and Mrs. White Owl.

Mr. White Owl said, "Susan had gone to see her friend, Pam Bernard, and they just disappeared."

Buff asked if the missing girls had anything in common. Mr. White Owl said, "No, nothing I can think of."

"Wait," Mrs. White Owl interrupted, "Both girls are on the Red Road. They go to all the ceremonies. They sweat every week. They have been to several Yuwipis and took part in the Sun Dance by dancing on the edge of the large circle. They all danced at pow-wows."

"Did any of the girls fight with each other?" Buff asked.

"No, they were best friends and never quarreled or fought," Mrs. White Owl said.

The other parents all agreed that there were no problems among the girls. Both parents painted the girls as being very spiritual. The girls went to the Catholic Church because they believed Jesus was the man and Christ the Consciousness.

Buff and Sandy went to Pine Ridge and searched for the girls every chance they got. But, the deputies didn't come up with a single clue. As time went by, less energy was being spent on finding the girls.

Buff called Randy Moore, his best friend in Afghanistan. Randy had been seriously wounded by an IED in Afghanistan. He spent a year in rehab. He then started training law enforcement dogs (Belgian Malinois). His training was the most extensive in the country. The dogs had to be able to track, search by smell, sniff out drugs, locate explosives and attack on verbal or hand commands and sniff out cadavers.

"Randy, how are you doing man?" Buff asked.

"I'm doing great and I love working with dogs," Randy said.

Buff asked if he had the perfect dog for him. Randy said, "Boy do I ever! I have an 85-pound Belgian Malinois that will graduate next week. He is military trained in attacking, tracking, sniffing out drugs, and finding cadavers. He's the best and sweetest dog I've ever trained, and he has titanium-capped canine teeth. I'm just afraid you won't be able to afford him. I'm asking $110,000. But for you, I'll sell him for $100,000."

"Give me your address and I'll have your $110,000 on the way. I've done pretty well for myself over the years."

"I'll need to come to your place for a week to show you how to work with him and for him to bond with you and follow your commands. You'll also have to build him a big training area. They have to be kept busy or you'll have trouble on your hands," Randy said.

"Okay. I'm looking forward to it," Buff agreed.

Buff called his contractor friend, John Lintz, to build him a training site in his ten acre backyard. The contractor built him an eight-foot-tall inverted V that had a 70-degree angle. Then they went to an open place. He placed eight large tractor tires on their sides with small car tires in between them. He dug holes and put the car tires facing up buried about one and a half feet down for the dog to crawl through.

John, on Buff's request, built a three-foot wall, a six-foot wall, an eight-foot wall, and an eight-foot-tall ladder with a slide at the top. He put in a thirty-foot-long tunnel made from culverts. He put in small posts two feet apart for the dog to weave through. He put in a teeter-totter. He hung a rope from a tree that was eight feet off the ground with a big knot in the end. His dog loved jumping up and grabbing it and shaking it.

Buff had a six-foot metal circle built with the capacity to fill with diesel and set on fire. It had a metal stand. He set it on fire and Lucky jumped right through the fire ring with just a little encouragement.

He decided to call the dog Lucky because he felt lucky to have this dog that was so well-trained.

Buff paid $1,700 for a bite training suit. He bought self-dispensing water and dog food bowls. He bought one eight-foot-long leash and a four-foot-long one. He also bought Lucky a thick collar and a bullet-proof vest for $4,000.

He called Randy and asked him if he could come up and stay with him for a week to turn Lucky over to Buff's commands. Randy said, "I'll be on the plane in the morning."

When Randy got there, Randy showed him Lucky's commands. Sit, down, attack, release and guard, search, heel, stay, come, find drugs, find bodies, track, and other commands. Lucky seemed to like Buff and they quickly bonded.

Randy said Lucky can run thirty-five miles an hour. His bite force is 1,400 pounds per square inch. With his titanium-capped canine teeth, he could bite deep into a subject and not break his teeth on the bones.

He said, "Lucky can pick up a scent under perfect conditions as far away as twenty kilometers." Lucky loved kids and they loved him.

Buff wondered how this lover could attack a man. Buff increased Lucky's training with the bite suit. He had friends come over and wear the bite suit so Lucky could get used to attacking other people rather than just going after him.

Buff bought Lucky a bulletproof vest with plates to stop even M-16s or AR-15s. He fell in love with that dog. He thought he'd die if he lost him.

Lucky could easily run at his eight-foot wall and push with his lower legs so he could get his front two legs over the top and climb over.

At the end of the week, Buff had control of Lucky. Buff thanked Randy and took him to the airport. Randy said, "You might have the best Belgian Malinois in the world."

Buff went to Sheriff Carlyle and told him all about Lucky. The sheriff said, 'Thank God you got such a great dog. You can start bringing him to work tomorrow. You'll have to get Sandy bonded with him too."

The next day, Sandy and Buff were on patrol with their new best friend, Lucky. They got a call that there was a fight at the Seventh Avenue Bar again. It took them only three minutes to get there.

Buff, Sandy, and Lucky stormed through the door. The fight was going strong. Everybody looked at the huge man, his partner, and the dog and they all froze in place. The fight was over.

"This is Lucky's first day on the job. Would any of you like to feel what a 1,400-pound bite force feels like?" Buff asked.

The bikers all started talking, and one biker said loudly, "No, we're done here - please don't let him loose on us."

"We will do whatever you want, Sheriff," another biker promised.

Buff pulled up the lips on Lucky's face and showed the bikers the titanium-capped canine teeth. Buff said, "I want every last one of you out of here within sixty seconds, and don't come back."

Back at home, Buff's dad Dawson took great pleasure in working with Lucky. He got an eight-foot long two inch thick rope and tied a big knot on each end. He got the dog to tug of war. He got Lucky to pull on the rope and then, after a minute, he let the brakes off of his wheelchair and Lucky would pull Dawson all over the huge yard. They both loved the game. He quickly fell in love with this incredible canine.

Buff and Sandy were heading down Mount Rushmore Road on their first night shift. They got a call that there was a burglary in progress at the Presidential Pawn Shop.

When they got to the scene they took a quick peek through the windows and saw two men flee out of the back door. Buff and Sandy ran around the building to the back. They saw two men running in opposite directions onto a field. Sandy said, "I'll get the one on the left because he's closest." She started running across the field and was quickly closing in on the fugitive.

Buff said to Lucky, "Takedown," and pointed at the other fleeing man. Running at thirty-five miles per hour, Lucky quickly overtook the man and bit down on the guy's right forearm. The man squealed in pain.

Buff came up to the man with the dog clamped on his arm and said, "release," and the dog immediately released the man. Buff said, "guard," and Lucky laid down next to the man. The dog's eyes stayed on the fugitive like lasers.

Sandy didn't take long to run down the other perp. She pushed the man in the back and the man sprawled onto his face. Sandy yelled, "Stay down," but the big guy threw Sandy off his back and pulled a huge knife from the sheath in his belt. Sandy jumped forward and kicked both of his knees and they folded back. The man screamed in pain.

They had the perps taken to Regional Hospital. The man whose knees were kicked in required extensive surgery. The other man yelled when they pushed medicine deep into his dog bite holes. He needed 19 stitches to close his dog bite wounds.

The man who had surgery on his knees had to spend 12 weeks in the hospital with daily physical therapy. He needed physical therapy for months after he got out of the hospital. After three months the men went to trial and both were found guilty of burglary and assault on police officers in the first degree.

Buff, Sandy, and Lucky went to the station to see Sheriff Carlyle. Carlyle's secretary, Becky Sashi, told them to go right in. The sheriff had his feet up on his desk and a big smile on his face. He said, "Good job on the takedown of the burglars. It looks like that dog of yours is going to be quite an asset to the department," he said, and then his tone changed.

"Listen, Sandy and Buff, the old religious cult compound that was shut down because the leader was a pedophile who arranged marriages for his men to marry 14-year-old girls was arrested and is now spending time in the state penitentiary at Sioux Falls."

"A shell company bought the compound that has an assortment of eighteen buildings. Some people were building fort-like walls around the compound. The corners were around twelve inches in diameter and ten feet tall. Old Man Mac, the head of the company building the fort walls, said he heard Harleys going in and out of there every night."

Carlyle said, "The only suspicious activity we know about so far are the bikers who go to the compound at night."

"We will do our best to find out what's going on out there," Sandy said.

"I'd like you two to do surveillance on the compound. Go to the bar that the workers are going to, and get all the information you can get. Be careful when you're scoping out the compound. Stay far away during the day so you can't be spotted using your binoculars. At night take your night vision goggles so you can get close."

In an unmarked car, Sandy, Buff, and Lucky drove out and got as close to the compound as they dared. They got out and found a comfortable place to lie down in the sand.

All they could see were workmen putting up the walls and a gate on the front side. They were well over halfway finished.

The next night, they went to check out the compound again. After two hours, 12 Harleys roared through the gate and into the compound. They didn't stay very long, but now Buff and Sandy saw who had hired workers to have the fort built.

The trio went back to the sheriff's office and told him what little they'd found out. Carlyle said, "I want you to go check on the compound weekly. Go to the Brass Rail Bar and see what information you can get from the workers."

Buff, Sandy, and Lucky walked into the bar and the place got quiet. Buff said, "We are not here to bust anyone. We're just looking for information. I'd like to speak to the man who is in charge of building the fort wall."

One of the men in the bar said, "Sure thing, I'm the boss at the compound. Ask any questions you'd like."

Buff introduced Lucky and Sandy, and the boss said, "Call me Mac. That's short for McCarthy."

Buff asked, "What can you tell me about the fort you're building?"

Mack said, "We were told it was going to be a tourist attraction."

Buff asked, "Have you seen anything strange out there?"

Mac said, "Yes. Every night, a bunch of rough-looking bikers go to the compound. I spent the night out there Thursday and watched the bikers. I have a strong feeling they're up to no good. I'm curious, is that a Belgian Malinois?"

Buff nodded Yes. Mac said, "I heard the Malinois is the best law enforcement canine in the world."

Buff said, "You won't get any argument from me."

Buff handed him a card and said, "Please call me if you see any more suspicious activity."

Mack said, "You got it."

Sheriff Carlyle got a call from the Pine Ridge Reservation Chief of Police. After his secretary, Becky transferred the call, she heard the sheriff ask, "What can I do for you?"

"We have two girls missing for over 24 hours again. We suspect foul play. Can you have Buff bring Lucky to the rez to track them?" the chief asked.

"Sure thing," said Carlyle and he hung up the phone. While he dialed Buff's mobile phone number he mumbled to himself, "Not again. We never found the last girls who went missing. But we didn't have Lucky on the force yet either. I'll pray for more luck this time."

Sandy, Buff, and Lucky went to Pine Ridge Reservation as soon as they could. They got some unwashed clothes that the girls had worn and Lucky got a good scent on all of them. Lucky was taken to where the girls were last seen and the dog alerted to their scent. He started pulling on his leash. Buff said, "Search!"

Lucky was soon tracking onto the edge of the area known as the Band Lands. After three miles they walked up a 15-foot spire and Lucky alerted Buff he was onto something. The dog went back down the spire to the other side. Buff had never seen Lucky so excited. Lucky went to the back of the spire and laid down on alert. There was a large cavern that sloped under the spire.

Buff and Sandy walked around the spire and used their flashlights to illuminate the largest crime scene that either of them had ever seen.

There were at least two dozen bodies in the cavern. Buff estimated that the most recent missing girls were the last bodies to have been slid into the cavern. They all had gunshot wounds to the backs of their heads.

Buff called the chief of police on the reservation and told him what he found. The chief said, "Now we know where most of the missing girls are. The young women and girls have been going missing since 1970."

Buff asked the chief to contact Search and Rescue, the medical examiner, and morticians. He told them to find guys with pickups to help transport the cadavers.

Buff called the Rapid City Chief of Police and asked him to secure the site until all the remains had been bagged and sent to Rapid City.

The medical examiner did the best he could to keep the bones of each body together. It was an impossible task.

Search and Rescue brought all the baskets they had. They brought searchlights, ropes, body bags, and extra manpower.

The sheriff's secretary, Becky, called some of the close surrounding communities and asked them if they could help. Within three hours there were about 50 workers and volunteers there. There were also dozens of four-wheel drive trucks.

It was decided that the medical examiner, a couple of police officers, and Buff would bag the two newest victims. As soon as they were bagged they went to Rapid City's morgue to get the autopsies started as soon as possible.

The Rapid City Medical Examiner said, "They were all shot in the back of their heads with a medium caliber pistol."

It took almost two days to get all the remains transported. They sent eight of them to the Sturgis Morgue because Rapid City Regional didn't have room for all of them.

The Pine Ridge Chief of Police called Buff and said, "I can't thank you enough. This will help give some closure to the families of all these deceased women. We can get DNA from their bones and identify all the bodies."

Buff and Sandy went to see the parents of the two most recently missing girls- the Sandmeiers and the Little Wolves.

Buff asked them to all come down to an interview room. Moving a little like robots, they followed Buff down the hall. He took them to the room and they all sat down around a plain wooden table. The parents looked shell-shocked. They sat still, staring into space.

Breaking the silence, Buff said, "I'm sorry for your loss. I know these questions will be hard, but I have to ask. Did Stacy or Teresa have any enemies?"

Mr. Sandmeier said, "Please call me Dennis. And no - Teresa had no enemies. She and her best friends followed the Red Road and they followed all the rules. Our two girls and sometimes three other girls joined them at the ceremonies."

Mrs. Little Wolf said, "No, Stacy was the sweetest girl in the world. My daughter also followed the red road and we all experienced almost all of the spiritual ceremonies together."

Dennis said, "I've participated in the Sun Dance four times and I pierced all four times. My daughter did a vision quest. She was very spiritual. They all went to the Catholic Church sometimes too, but they said, "It helps us remember that Jesus was the man, and Christ the Consciousness."

Buff was now convinced the murders had something to do with the Red Road and Buff and Sandy were determined to catch the culprit.

Later, Buff, Sandy, and Lucky went door to door to ask the neighbors if they saw or heard anything about the dead girls. It was Buff's turn to go up to the next house.

Sandy stayed in the SUV parked down the street and gave Lucky food and water. Buff walked up to the front door. He saw a woodcrafted sign that said "Sanders" on it. The Sanders had a nice home with a manicured yard with lots of bushes, shrubs, and flowery plants.

Bud Sanders came out to greet him. Bud was of average height and weight. He had brown hair and a very pale complexion. He was smoking a cigarette when he opened the door, and quickly put it out against the door jamb when he saw Buff.

"Hi," began Buff. "I'm a Pennington County Sheriff's Deputy."

"I'm Bud Sanders, and it's nice to meet you," Bud answered. "Please, come in!"

Buff made note that Bud sounded a little nervous. He stated right off, "I'm checking around the neighborhood to see if anyone knows about any girls going missing from the area."

"No, Sheriff, I don't think so."

Buff asked Bud Sanders, "Hey, I'm curious. How do you feel about what they call the Red Road?"

Bud said, "That heathen Red Road with the bad spirits is the road to perdition."

They now had a suspect. Buff smelled the sour scent of the murderer. He excused himself and said goodbye to Bud.

Sandy, Buff and Lucky went together to interview Bud again the next day. "Welcome sheriffs and the beautiful canine. Come in please."

Buff said, "These are my partners, Sandy, and Lucky."

Bud "goo gooed," at the dog as though he were a baby as they walked into the house.

They settled in the living room and Bud asked if they wanted something to drink. Sandy said, "Please, anything wet will do."

Bud went to get her a bottle of water and came back quickly to hand it to her. Sandy said, "Thank you very much."

Buff asked Bud if he had any family living with him. Bud answered, "No, I have no one now. My wife left me and took our kid with her almost a year ago. My kid used to hang out with those Indians."

"Really?" Buff asked. "I would like to know more about how you feel about the Red Road. I think we may have found something in common."

"Well, I hesitate to say how much I hate it and being this close to it," Bud said,."I'm a Catholic and I don't want to be around those evil spirits the medicine man calls in. My kid kept running off to join whatever cult they were a part of. That's how I saw how evil they are."

"I see! You saw all that crazy stuff that happens there, first hand," Buff commented hoping to encourage Bud to keep talking.

"She was always sneaking off to ceremonies anyway, it was hard to keep up with her, but I was determined to save her and all the other young girls who went there," Bud admitted.

"I don't blame you, I don't like it either," Buff said. Sandy was standing behind Bud and raised her eyebrow at her partner.

Bud continued, excited to have found someone to talk to about it. "I believe the Red Road is Satan's path. My God, they get pierced by the medicine man and they dance for three and a half days and then tear their flesh to finish the ceremony. How sick is that?"

After they left Bud's home, Buff said to Sandy, "I think Bud is killing those women. There is something wrong with that angry man."

Sandy said, "I agree, we've got to set a trap for him."

Buff asked, "What kind of trap do you propose?"

"You're the boss so you're supposed to figure it out," Sandy said.

The Pine Ridge Police Chief called Buff to report, "We've had four young men murdered on the reservation. I'm sure they were meth dealers but I could never catch them with that shit. I think somebody is trying to take over the meth trade." Buff thought of the just-finished fort.

The chief continued, "I got a call from a young Lakota man. He reported that all the meth dealers on Pine Ridge Reservation had been warned by rough-looking bikers that they better start working for them, or they'll all end up dead. He said many of them gave up and went to the Fort when it was finished to work for the bikers."

"The young man said he went to work for them so he could spy on them and report their doings to law enforcement when he found something solid. He found out that they have a huge meth lab in operation and they're all armed with AR-15s plus they all have pistols. It seems that they easily took over the meth trade on the rez. Meth is ruining our communities. The young man said he became an informant because he wanted to do all he could to help take them down."

"Do these bikers have a name?" Buff asked, angrily making a fist with the hand that wasn't holding his phone.

"The young man said that they call themselves Satan's Spawn. He learned that they tried to take over part of the Bandidos and the Hells Angels' territories but after five of their members were killed, they started looking for a safer place, and they found the Pine Ridge Reservation. The abandoned cult buildings were perfect. They could easily make enough meth for the nearly 9,000 men, women, and children on the Reservation, and get them all addicted to meth. After they got established, they were going to expand to Rapid City where there are already thousands of meth users. This young man put himself in terrible danger to learn all this. I trust him."

With Buff's leadership, the Rapid City Police Department, the Pennington County Sheriff's Department, and the Pine Ridge Reservation Police decided to join forces and fight the meth epidemic on and off the reservation.

Meth was everywhere, and quite a few people died when they got some meth mixed with fentanyl. They wouldn't be feeling anything, again. Most estimates say at least 40% of the local adults and kids on the reservation were hooked on meth, which is almost 5,000 people.

After talking to all the law enforcement heads for hours on the phone, they decided to get every possible person to come to the complex and shut it down.

Buff said, "This probably is going to be the only time we'll have a chance to shut down most of the meth trade here. I want all your input and I'll tell you about the plan I have. It's going to be a huge operation. First of all, they are all armed with AR-15s. I was told that we can borrow enough confiscated AR-15s from Rapid City Police and the Sioux Falls Police Departments. I'd like to have all six of the highway patrolmen bring their Belgian Malinois. And of course, I'll bring my dog, Lucky."

"I'd like the highway patrol officers to have their dogs in the forest, two in the back and two on each side. I'll have Lucky in the front with me. Any runners will have to run about 150 yards to reach the forest. Have your dogs take them down just ten yards from the trees. The other 12 Highway Patrol officers will hide in the trees to the south."

"We'd like the state police and the Box Elder Police to be hidden in the trees to the east. The sheriff's deputies will take the front. The Sioux Falls Sheriff's department will have their men on the west. The Rapid City S.W.A.T. team with their armored vehicle will drive straight up to about 50 yards from the compound's door."

"I'll have planted C-4 explosives on all four corners of the walls, and smaller amounts all around the fort's walls all hooked up to one detonator. Thanks to the Rapid City Police Department for the large amount of C-4 that they had confiscated a couple of years ago. Good thing homeland security never bothered to pick it up."

"I'm sure they'll fight because they are not expecting 77 of us. There are probably 80-90 bikers in the compound. Make sure your shots count. I've got 20 guys with 20 trucks with hitches on them. I've deputized them and at 3 A.M., I want those trucks to back up to the walls where I asked them to. They'll lasso the sharpened posts and attach them to their trucks' hitches. That will be five trucks on each side, all evenly spaced apart. Any questions?"

"Are we going to have enough ammunition for the AR-15s?" asked a state trooper.

"We'll have enough ammo for twice as many men that we have. Each person will have 8 30-round magazines. I really doubt you'll need that many clips, but shoot only if you have to. Any more questions?

"No more questions? So we will meet up at the old drive-in theater by the fort."

Two nights later at 3:00 A.M., about 60 vehicles including five ambulances, two buses, and dozens of law enforcement vehicles, and the 20 newly deputized pickup truck drivers arrived at the compound. Buff told the pickup drivers that after they pulled the fort walls down after the C-4 exploded that they needed to go to the edge of the trees and turn their trucks around and turn on their bright lights.

The trucks backed up to the walls and the men threw their lassos over the tops of the pointed posts.

"Start after I get about twenty-five yards from the compound and I'll yell in my bullhorn," Buff said.

Buff figured they'd have a big gun battle, Buff yelled into the bullhorn, "Surrender. You are surrounded and you're all under arrest. We have you surrounded. Give up, Come out with your hands on top of your heads." Nobody came out.

Everybody waited for the C-4 to go off. Buff clicked the detonator and the C-4 detonated all around the compound. The pickups pulled the walls down and then raced to the trees. They turned their trucks around to point their headlights at the action.

The walls came down beautifully including the front wall with the gate.

Semi-automatic and automatic gunfire erupted from the compound. Buff had warned everybody not to shoot at all into the big brown building that housed the meth lab. They didn't need a big explosion.

Buff's men opened up and they were shredding the wooden structures in the compound. Six men took a run for the forest and the dogs took down the fugitives right where they were supposed to. The men were screaming and the dog handlers said, "Release and guard."

The dogs all laid down and kept their eyes on the runners. The highway patrolmen quickly handcuffed the men.

A sheriff's deputy said, "There goes another runner." Sure enough, there was a guy running, who stopped to try and hijack one of the pickup trucks. The doors were locked and he wasted time trying to punch out a window. The driver inside ignored his demands.

Lucky was already watching the guy because it's where Buff was looking; he pointed at the fugitive and said loudly, "TAKE DOWN."

The man had reached the forest and had climbed twenty feet up a pine tree. Lucky easily climbed the tree and clamped down on the man's calf. The man screamed, "I give up! Please get him off me!"

Buff said, "Release!" Lucky released the man's leg and jumped down. The man crawled part way down and then fell the rest of the way. He landed in the leaves in front of the tree. Lucky was still watching him.

Buff handcuffed the man, grinning from ear to ear. It had somehow slipped his mind that Malinois could climb trees.

The battle in the compound raged for ten minutes. Then, some of the bikers started shouting, "We surrender!"

The living bikers were all cuffed with plastic ties. Some of the un-injured were taken to prison buses and handcuffed to the floor. There were 60 bikers alive and 25 bikers dead. Many of the still living had serious gunshot wounds. The most seriously injured were put in the ambulances and they were zip tied to the gurneys' railings. They sped away with lights on and sirens blaring. The other wounded were laid down in the back of the pickup trucks with a law enforcement officer.

The ambulances and trucks were heading for Regional Hospital in Rapid City.

The seven men with dog bites had to be taken to Regional's ER as well, because serious dog bites usually cause life-threatening infections unless rigorously treated.

Buff called the medical examiners and they all went to the morgue. Buff called the Sturgis Police Department and asked how much room they had for prisoners in their cells. The man told him we have room for twenty. He then called Pennington County Jail and they said they could take thirty prisoners. They weren't too busy. There was room for everybody.

At the compound, they dealt with the 25 dead bikers. It took them all day to canvas the scene. They had to bag over 80 AR-15s and over 70 pistols and their ammo. Sandy took pictures before any of the dead were removed. Sandy was invaluable.

Buff took Lucky back to what was left of the fort. He took him to the big brown building and Lucky alerted and lay down in front of the door. Buff carefully entered the building and was shocked. The bikers had at least 800 pounds of meth, a couple of big bags of cocaine, and hundreds of pounds of pot with a few large bags of fentanyl.

Buff's crew only had one seriously injured man. He was a highway patrolman with a shot in his gut. Ten of his people had minor wounds and were soon patched up.

The raid was national news for several days. It would take a year or more for all the trials to be finished. They all were charged with attempted murder, murder, and making and selling of controlled substances as well as other charges.

Buff decided to take a few days off and train and play with his dog. He put Lucky through the obstacle course. He also decided to teach Lucky how to do a back flip. Buff took a bunch of dog treats. He held the treat close to the ground and Lucky sniffed it. Buff then held the treat a little higher than Lucky could reach.

Lucky jumped up and grabbed it. Buff then held the treat as high as he could and a little back of Lucky's head. Lucky jumped and missed the treat. Buff kept at it for a couple of hours. He was just going to quit for the day and decided he would try one more time. Buff quickly lowered the treat from the ground to high above and slightly behind where Lucky's head would be when he jumped.

Lucky jumped, threw his head back and grabbed the treat, and threw his body back and over. Buff did it a couple more times and Lucky did perfectly each time. Lucky could now do a back flip. Buff decided to teach Lucky another trick.

The next day his friend Mike Voltz came over to watch Buff teach Lucky. They went into the living room and placed two recliners face to face about three feet apart. Buff ordered Lucky to jump onto his recliner and sit. Lucky did so. Buff took a treat and told Lucky to hug. He patted his legs and chest. Lucky jumped into Buff's lap and took the treat.

Buff then had Lucky stand in front of him and he held a treat to his chest and said, "Hug." Lucky jumped into Buff's chest and Buff handed him the treat. He practiced the hug command for an hour.

Buff then had Lucky stand 25 yards away from him and he yelled, "Hug," and Lucky ran quickly to Buff and threw himself sideways against Buff's chest. What a smart, amazing dog, Buff thought.

Buff sent the Pine Ridge Reservation one million dollars for them to expand their drug and alcohol treatment programs. They could use any money left over for whatever they thought they needed the money for the most.

A few days later Buff got a call about three missing teenage boys. Buff called the parents and asked them to come to his office with some dirty clothes or a hairbrush for Lucky to smell. One set of parents said, "They had gone cave crawling or spelunking." The other parents weren't told where their son was going.

Buff asked the parents where their sons usually went cave crawling. They all said, "Dark Canyon."

Buff said, "I have a really good idea where they are. I hope I'm right. I used to spelunk in Dark Canyon when I was a youngster. There is one place that is easy to get trapped in, but I am too big to squeeze through a very narrow passage.

Buff, Sandy, and Lucky led the way to Brook's Cave in Dark Canyon. Someone had put metal gates to close the cave to the public, but kids always managed to tear the gates off.

When they got to Brook's Cave, Lucky alerted and lay down at the entrance. Buff said to Sandy, "I can't fit through the very tight space - you have to crawl through to reach the 10' cliff inside. You'll fit through there easily." Buff then called Pennington County Search and Rescue to bring ropes, a rope ladder and a medical bag. He also asked them to bring some small guys or women to get through the cave.

Sandy said, "You didn't ask me if I'm afraid of dark or narrow places."

Buff asked, "Well, are you?"

Sandy said, "No. I used to go cave crawling with my brothers. I loved it."

Buff yelled into the cave, "Is anyone there?"

There was no answer. He said, "They're probably too far away for any of them to hear us. They might be trapped at the bottom of the 10-foot drop-off."

Sandy asked Buff for his flashlight. She said, "When we went cave crawling we all had to have two lights. Sometimes we'd use carbide lanterns as one source of light."

Buff gave Sandy his flashlight and told her, "You'll go in straight for about 30 yards, and then you'll reach the narrowing of the cave. You should have no problem getting through that. The cave then turns to the left and about sixty yards later you'll reach the cliff."

Sandy crawled into the narrow entrance and soon was at the drop-off. She saw a broken rope piece at the top. The worn out rope had been there for years and had finally snapped. Sandy yelled, "Anyone here?"

She immediately heard three voices yelling, "Help! We're here!" She shined her light down the cliff and the three youngsters were all right at the bottom of the wall.

Sandy asked, "Is anyone hurt?"

One of the boys said, "Toby has a broken leg."

He said, "It's on the lower right leg and a piece of one of his bones is sticking through his jeans."

Sandy said, "We call that a tib-fib compound fracture. I know you're in a lot of pain, but Search and Rescue will soon put on a traction splint and your pain level will drop significantly."

Sandy crawled out of the cave and filled Buff in. Buff called for an ambulance. Search and Rescue got to the cave a minute before the ambulance. Sandy filled the ambulance crew and the Search and Rescue team in about what she saw and they developed a plan. Two Search and Rescue team members crawled into the cave with a splint, a coil of rope, and a rope ladder. They soon reached the 10-foot drop off. The Search and Rescue team consisted of two women. They climbed down the ladder and applied the traction splint to Toby's leg.

Toby said, "Man, that feels so much better."

Search and Rescue used some of the rope to truss up Toby so they could pull him up the cliff. Two of the Search and Rescue team members climbed down the ladder and prepared to haul Toby up. They lifted him so his back was against the cliff. The rescuers pulled him up and Toby screamed as they pulled his legs over the top of the cliff.

An ambulance crew member came up to the top of the cliff. He said, "You shouldn't feel too much pain because I'm going to give you a shot with 4 mg of morphine." The rescuers tied a rope to Toby's harness and started to drag him out of the cave. Tobey had moaned a few times but apparently, the morphine was doing its job.

When they got Toby out, Search and Rescue put him in a rescue basket and carried him the half-mile walk to the ambulance. The ambulance took off with lights and siren.

They had Tim and James climb the rope ladder and crawl out of the cave. The sheriff notified the parents and they were extremely happy and thankful.

Buff said, "Come Sandy and Lucky."

Sandy said, "If you talk to me like I'm a dog again you'd better be ready to use your gun."

Buff said, "Jeez, can't you take a joke?"

"Usually, but I guess I just want to shoot you."

Buff said, "Thanks, Sandy. You know how to make a man feel great - I love you too!"

Buff got home at 11 P.M. Vera was waiting for him.

When he saw her, Buff said, "You need your sleep - You shouldn't still be up. I noticed that you've lost weight and you don't look well."

Vera said, "I want you to go for a sweat with me tomorrow. On Sunday, I'd like you to come to the Catholic Church with me. Dawson will be there too."

Buff said, "You know I'm not much on religion."

Vera said, "Your father and I really need you to come."

"Are you sick?"

"I'll tell you everything at church."

Buff went to church with Vera and his dad. During the service, the pastor said, "Vera would like to talk to all of us. Come on up to the lectern, Vera."

Vera went up and said. "Metakuye Oyiasin (all my relatives).

The congregation all answered, "Metakuye Oyiasin"

Vera said, "I know this is highly irregular but I've got stage IV breast cancer and I only have a couple of months left, if I'm lucky."

Sitting in the pews, Dawson sucked in a breath, and Buff put his hand across Dawson's shoulders in support. "My dearest husband, and my son, Buff, I hope you'll understand why I told you this way, but you know I've always done things my way when possible and I need your help. If anyone else here wants to visit me, do it now because I don't want to visit with anyone but Buff and Dawson when I'm on my deathbed."

"The day after I'm gone please go to the Catholic Church's gym and bring casseroles, drinks, and any other food to celebrate my memory."

"Buff, I want you to build a scaffold for me. I want to be put on the scaffold wearing my beautiful black dress and wrapped with scarves. On the anniversary of my death, I'd like you to fill the space under the scaffold with split, dried pine logs and light it. After the fire is completely out I'd like you to bury my bones close by in a very small grave. Take away any unburned wood, and then rake my ashes over the area so that it will soon look undisturbed."

Two months and one week later Vera died. Buff had already built her a ten-foot-tall platform. He used six-by-six posts on the corners and two by six boards for the flooring. A huge crowd gathered as they placed Vera on the scaffold that was about 200 yards away from their log home.

Joe, one of Buff's best friends, asked, "You know that's illegal to build a scaffold and put a body on it don't you? She's gonna be up there for a whole year, chances are someone will see it in all that time."

Buff said, "They can all go fuck themselves if they don't like it. Besides, I can't believe any of Vera's friends would tell anybody." Buff went to the scaffold every day, sometimes with Dawson. They both felt lost and broken to pieces.

After a few days, Buff told Sheriff Carlyle that he was going to the Pine Ridge Reservation for a couple of weeks. The Pine Ridge Police had called him and asked for help in arresting the killer of those dozens of women. He knew if he didn't work, he'd go crazy so he decided to go help. Sandy volunteered to go with him and he agreed.

When they got to the reservation, Buff and Sandy left Lucky in the car with all the windows down, and it wasn't too hot so Lucky would be fine. They went to see the Sandweiers and the Little Wolves to talk again. The Little Wolf family and the Sandweiers were still totally devastated, but they said they had racked their brains and still had no clue who had killed the girls.

Buff and Sandy did have clues that pointed to Bud Sanders. Buff asked Sandy if he should interview the suspect one more time, alone? The guy might open up more or even get rough during the interview.

Sandy agreed. Buff went up to the nice house and knocked. Bud answered the door and said, "Hello Sheriff. Good to see you. Did you come to visit again?"

"Well, we don't have much yet on the case. I wanted to talk to you again. I think we could be friends."

"Sure, I'll make us some tea," Bud offered.

"Oh, no thanks, I have water out in the vehicle that I've been drinking all morning," Buff said. He didn't trust Bud not to poison him. He was still smiling with a friendly face.

Buff discreetly turned on the voice recorder hidden in his pocket and said, "I've never told anyone else this, but I sense a kindred spirit. All the people following the Red Path are on their way to hell, but even they don't know it. The Red Path is like a peach - sweet and inviting, but inside is rotten with worms." Buff smiled as he spoke.

"Yeah - I know this too - It's nice to know you think so. You'll understand my pain. I tried to get my ex-wife to stop going, but she refused," Bud explained. Feeling closer to the deputy Sheriff, Bud patted Buff's broad shoulder and invited him to sit down in the dining area with a motion of his hand.

Buff said, "Did you know they call in spirits during their ceremonies? They are evil! I only believe in God and the Holy Spirit. Jesus was the man, and Christ the Consciousness."

"I've never heard it put that way, but it sounds right on. There is only one true God," Bud said.

"Exactly. We know the way. I hate the Red Road and can't believe how so many can be attracted to it. For Christ's sake, they pierce themselves, tie themselves to something, and after three days, they have to rip their own skin to get free!" Buff said, with all the feeling he could muster.

"But Buff, ain't you part injun yourself?" Bud asked, sounding a little accusatory.

Buff said, "Yeah, but I don't believe in their spirits or practices. How do you feel about all the Native women found dead recently?"

"They only got what they deserved," Bud said, smiling. "Maybe we could work together."

"Sure, I like you, but work together on what?" Buff asked. "I'll help you with whatever you ask."

"Do you swear to God almighty that you're not trying to set me up?" Bud asked.

Buff said, "I swear."

"Okay, hypothetically, I would lure these girls to an old burial ground as an excuse," Bud said.

"How would you get all those girls to walk up to the spire?" Buff asked boldly.

"I told them we'd get a good view of the old burial ground from the top of the spire." Bud sounded like he wasn't speaking hypothetically anymore.

"Keep up the good work. You're doing God's work," Buff said. "Let me know when, and I'll help you."

"I had you all wrong, Sheriff. You're a great man.

"Do you have any plans to kill any more girls, soon?" Buff asked directly, thinking that Bud was off his guard.

"I have two girls who already want to go with me to the burial site. But since the other girls' bodies were found, I guess I've got to find a new place to dispose of the bodies," Bud said matter of fact.

"Yes, I guess you will," Buff said. "Hey, my partner just texted me. She is waiting for me to go to eat lunch with her. I'll see you later."

"Keep in touch, Sheriff," Bud said.

Practically skipping with joy, Buff ran to the Bronco, and Sandy was sleeping with her head against the window. Buff opened the driver's door and jumped in. He said, "Rise and shine."

Sandy rose sleepily and while yawning, she stretched her arms to the windshield. Buff told her, "I've got something you've got to hear."

Sandy said, "I hope it's good."

"It's great! Just listen! Then give me your take on it," Buff said. He rolled up all the windows and turned on the AC. He backed up a bit to be sure they couldn't be seen or heard from the home he'd just left. Buff played the recording.

"He really did confess. I can't believe he would say that to a sheriff he hardly knows." Sandy said.

"He's proud of what he's done, he thinks he is doing right and wants to brag about it to someone," Buff suggested. "He didn't even take much convincing that I was on his side."

"We can get a search warrant now," Sandy said.

Buff drove straight to the judge. After he heard the tape too, he said, "You've got yourself a search warrant. Arrest Sanders for murder and then do the search for solid evidence."

Buff, Sandy, and Lucky with four other Deputies gathered and left to execute the arrest and search warrant.

Buff, and Sandy, kicked the door down. Bud fell off of a kitchen chair in surprise. "Hey! What's going on?" Bud asked.

Buff keyed his mic and told the others to come into the house. He pulled out his .44 magnum and pointed it at Bud, telling him to sit in the living room in a chair by the wall and not to move. He handed the search warrant to Bud.

Then the other Deputies got to the house. Buff said, "Sandy, arrest Bud for suspicion of murder and cuff him. The rest of you tear this house apart until you find the gun. Do the same with the garage and shed out back. I know it's here."

Bud screamed angrily, "You fucking liar!"

"Yes, and it's my pleasure where you're concerned," Buff answered, smiling.

The deputies took turns guarding Bud. Sandy and the others started tearing the place apart as ordered. Just when they were ready to quit, Sandy noticed something not quite right about the flooring in the closet. One board was about 3/8 of an inch taller than the rest of the flooring.

Sandy went to the bathroom and found a big pair of scissors. She pushed the scissors into the crack and raised the board. A gun and ammunition were in the space under the floor.

Sandy called everybody to come up and showed them her find. They very carefully put the gun and ammo in separate evidence bags.

They loaded Bud into the back seat of the sheriff's Bronco. The sheriff read him his rights. Buff asked a deputy to get in the back seat with him and move Bud's cuffed hands behind his back.

When they got to the jailhouse, they pushed Bud into a cell after setting his hands free. The cell had a camera in it and they put Bud on suicide watch.

Bud said, "You promised God that you were telling me the truth."

"Sorry, I follow the Red Road and law enforcement can lie to suspects all they want."

Bud said, "You're going to hell!"

Buff said, "I sincerely doubt it."

Ballistics verified that the gun they found was used on all those dead Lakota women. All but three of the bodies had been identified. The tribe presented Buff with an eagle feather that was legally obtained.

The Lakota and Dakota believe that eagle feathers possess spirit and power. Eagles are the closest connection people can have with God.

They danced for two hours at the pow-wow. They had a great feast that included buffalo roasts. People came from all over the country. It was huge national news. Buff was interviewed and decided he'd tell them almost everything. Right after Buff was done, all the news people disappeared.

The trial for Bud was a short one, and the jury came in with unanimous guilty verdicts in four hours. Everyone in the courtroom cheered and clapped except for the judge. He didn't admonish the crowd. He thanked the jurors, released them, and said, "Bud Sanders - you'll be sentenced in twenty-five days from today. We are adjourned."

Twenty-five days later as promised, the judge ordered Bud Sanders to spend the rest of his life in prison. The large crowd clapped and cheered again. The parents and families felt some relief from their terrible tragedies and watched the prisoner in shackles being taken away.

A few days later, dispatch called Buff and told him that apparently, two teenagers had drowned at Sheridan Lake.

"One of them was struggling to get back to the beach. He went under and his friend went to save him. His friend found him and started to pull him back to shore. The boy that had been drowning grabbed onto his friend's arms and they disappeared together," the dispatcher said. "And we were told that you have one of the few dogs that can smell 30 feet down in the water, is that true?"

"Yes, he's trained to sniff out bodies underwater. I'd like you to get a boat or rubber raft where Lucky can stand at the bow. Also call the medical examiner, two Search and Rescue divers, and two ambulances," Buff instructed, confident that Lucky would find them. "Sandy, Lucky and I will be there in about thirty minutes."

When they reached the site, Buff saw a huge rubber raft with two Search and Rescue responders sitting on the raft. "That will work perfectly," Buff thought.

Buff had Lucky get to the front of the large rubber raft. He stayed right behind him. He told Lucky to "find the bodies." They trolled around Sheridan Lake.

After 20 minutes, Lucky alerted Buff by standing up, whining and looking over the side of the rubber raft. The divers went down and searched the murky water. Finally, one diver bumped into a body and brought it up. The other diver soon found the other body.

They took the bodies into a tent that Search and Rescue had erected. The four parents came down to the tent and asked if they could look at the bodies of their sons.

"You don't have to. We can ID the boys by DNA," Buff said. The parents still wanted to see the bodies.

After the parents had looked at their sons one of the mothers came up to Buff, sobbing. She grabbed Buff in a bear hug with her arms around his waist. She said, "Thank you so much for finding our boy."

The other woman did the same soon after. The boys' fathers came up and shook Buff's hands. It was a really bittersweet feeling Buff had. They took the bodies to the morgue.

It had been one year to the day since Vera died, and Buff invited everybody to witness Vera's cremation.

He walked up to the scaffolding and took out a knife. He cut his left cheek deeply to match the scar on his other cheek. It used to be a common practice for the Lakota tribe to cut themselves while they were mourning. He let blood drip on the split pine logs under the scaffolding. The fire took off and quickly it surrounded the scaffold.

After about five hours the fire was out except for only a few smoldering pieces of wood. In the middle of the burned area were Vera's bones. Buff's friends buried Vera's bones in a small grave not far from where the pyre had been. Others removed the unburned logs and threw them in the back of a truck. His other friends raked and raked the area to fully scatter the ashes. Vera had wanted to have the site looking undisturbed in only a year or two.

Vera's death made Buff think a lot about his life and the possibility of his own family. Vera had told him that she thought he should get married as soon as possible. He'd just laugh it off, but now, Sandy was so beautiful and smart and such a good partner that he was sure that he was falling in love with her.

At home Buff looked all over the house for his father. He nearly panicked when he found him. He was lying in the bathroom, his chair on its side. "Dad!" Buff cried as he ran over.

"I'm okay son, I just got stuck and couldn't pull myself back into the chair."

"How long have you been like this?" Buff asked.

"I'm not sure. Only a couple of hours I think." Buff had his father back into his chair and had pushed him out into the bedroom. He sat on the foot of the bed to talk to Dawson.

"Oh God! I'm so glad I didn't have to work longer today!"

"I guess this is a good time to tell you," Dawson began.

"Tell me what?"

"Well, my sister and brother in law have invited me to go to Seattle and live with them. My sister is home most of the time taking care of their two kids, and they could use my help. For the last year, I've been here alone most of the time. I think it would be for the best."

"I think so too, but I will miss you, dad."

Buff got his father a plane ticket and helped him to the airport and onto the plane. His sister and brother in law met him at the Seattle airport.

Buff, Sandy, and Lucky went to a casino robbery in progress. Buff and Lucky went to the front door. Sandy went to the back door and tried the door handle. She found it locked; so Sandy did a flying kick to the door and it opened a little. She kicked it again and she was in.

"Sheriff's department - you are under arrest," she yelled.

The two robbers tried to run out the back door. Buff knocked the first one out with a jumping front kick. The other robber still ran toward the back.

Buff pointed at the man and told Lucky, "Take down."

The man saw the dog running after him and he put out his hands to try to stop the dog. Lucky clamped down on the man's hand and his bones made a snapping sound. He screamed and went to his knees.

"Let go! Let go!" he cried.

Walking up to the man, Buff said, "Release."

Lucky immediately let go and laid down where he was. Buff cuffed the man and then he called for an ambulance. Sandy came through the back door and asked, "Is everything okay?"

Buff instructed her, "Zip-tie the knocked out guy and have dispatch send two cars to transport them."

The ambulances arrived and Buff took a good look at the man's hand. The only word to describe it was *mangled*.

The man that Buff took down was still unconscious. One of the ambulances took him to the ER for treatment.

Buff drove for a few miles and Sandy asked, "Where are we going?"

Buff said, "Right here," as he pulled over.

"Sandy, I don't know how you'll feel about this, but here goes. I love you and want to marry you. I didn't get a ring yet, because I didn't know how you were going to take this. If you say yes, I'll buy you a big diamond." Buff rambled on and on, not giving her a chance to speak.

Sandy slid over and planted an extremely passionate kiss on Buff's mouth. They made out for 20 minutes before they came up for air.

"Your house or mine?" Sandy said.

"Mine," Buff answered quickly.

They got to Buff's house and Sandy said, "I'm going to take a quick shower."

Buff said, "How about we save water?"

"Sounds great," Sandy said, getting his meaning.

Buff got in the shower with her and washed her hair. He gently washed the rest of her from her toes to her face. Sandy washed Buff, and she spent quite a lot of time below his waist. Sandy dried off and went to bed, and Buff was soon beside her. "Anything special you want?" he asked.

"Just you," Sandy answered, using her deepest, sexiest voice.

They started making very slow, passionate love. Just before Buff was ready to cum he stopped until he was sure he wasn't going to cum. Few other men could have done it.

It was especially hard for him to hold back because she was running her hands over his belly and chest and playing with his nipples. They were all over each other. Buff never felt so good. Sandy came several times.

Two hours later Buff couldn't hold it any more. He said to Sandy, "Are you ready to cum with me?"

"Yes, Yes - Yes!" Sandy answered urgently.

Buff started really pounding her and soon they both cried out when they climaxed.

Panting, Buff asked Sandy, "Can we go get a ring in the morning?"

Sandy panted. "Yes, and I know a judge who can marry us tomorrow afternoon," Sandy added, still panting. She took a deep breath and said, "Let's do this!"

The next morning, Buff went and bought Sandy a two carat solitaire diamond. That afternoon, with just a couple of close friends attending, they got married.

"I've never been so happy in my life," Sandy whispered to Buff.

Even after a couple of months, Sandy thought about how his love making was perfect. She loved it that Buff always started slowly and gave her multiple orgasms. The best was when they climaxed together.

A few weeks later while they were out on patrol, the dispatcher came on and asked, "Are you there, Deputy Means?"

Buff answered, "Sure am, what's going on?"

The dispatcher said, "We have a robbery at Sam's Pizza."

Buff, Sandy and Lucky hurried to the robbery. Buff stopped at the side of the pizza place, arriving first. Buff jumped out and crept low to stay out of sight of anyone inside. He tried the door and found it open. He motioned Sandy to go to the back door.

Buff went in and said, "Stay where you are - we don't want to have to shoot you."

The man ran toward the back door, slammed it open and ran out. Sandy yelled, "Get on the ground with your hands ..."

But even before she finished yelling he turned to run to the tree line that marked the edge of the forest. Sandy ran after him, and was quickly overtaking him. The robber turned around with a gun pointed right at Sandy.

The armed robber shot two times, and missed both times. Sandy shot at him twice. She put a bullet in his chest and another in his forehead. He dropped like a rock. Sandy ran to him to be sure he was dead, although on her way, she thought there was no way he would still be alive.

When she got a closer look, she could tell right away that she had just shot a teenager. Tears welled up in her eyes. She fought to keep from crying and ran back around front where another patrol car had just rolled up.

Inside, Buff found an 18-21 year old boy dead on the pizza place's floor. He had two shots in his chest. Another patrol car pulled up and Sandy asked the officer to keep watch over the dead burglar; so no one would disturb the scene.

Sandy went inside to talk to Buff. As soon as she saw him she ran to him and wrapped her arms around him. She was sobbing and said, "I just killed a teenager!"

"It's not your fault. That teenager killed another teenager first and he would have killed you or any of us too."

Sandy stopped crying while listening to Buff's comforting words. She sniffled once and called the medical examiner.

By then seven Sheriff and police cars were all out front with their lights blazing.

The medical examiner told Buff and Sandy that it looked like a closed case. But that's not how things work with the police. Once back at the station, they took Sandy to an interrogation room and she told them what had happened. They took her pistol and shield. They told her she was on leave for two weeks.

Sandy stayed home for the two weeks except for going to the grocery store twice. When Buff got home one afternoon, he asked Sandy to sit down and listen to him.

"You've been a deputy for ten years now," Buff said.

"Seems like twenty, but yes."

"I have a proposition for you. I want you to quit the sheriff's department with me and start a new endeavor. Since we both have more than ten years in law enforcement, we can carry our weapons anywhere in the country," Buff said. "I'd like to start up a new company. I have my eye on a 2011 Beechcraft twin engine that has room for six. I've asked an instructor, John Stires, to fly for us and teach us how to fly ourselves; so we can both get our Pilot's licenses." The offer was too good for her to turn down.

"I want to fly all over the country to small towns when they need a trained dog. I also want to have Lucky find the remains of Native Americans who have been buried at boarding schools since the 1880s. They finally closed the last schools in 1991."

"I'm going to try to get a hold of all law enforcement personnel that have cadaver dogs and ask them to check their state's old boarding schools. On those sites where the old schools used to be before they were torn down. So far they have recovered the remains of 500 Native American youngsters. There are probably thousands of unmarked graves all over the United States."

"I've got a lot of law enforcement friends, and I think I can start a national movement to find most of the youth buried in unmarked graves. There were 408 Indian boarding schools."

"That sounds like a wonderful service. And I know how you've always found a way to help people. I will get a pilot's license too?" Sandy excitedly asked to confirm.

"Yes, of course," Buff said.

"Let's get started," Sandy said.

They gave the sheriff's office two weeks' notice. The sheriff said he could work until fall and if he wanted to work for free he could stay on the force.

"Let's go to Rapid City Regional Airport," Buff said.

They had several hangers there for lease but Buff wanted to go look at the plane for sale first. It was a twin-engine 2011 six-passenger Beechcraft airplane that he was very excited about. Buff called the owner and the owner said, "I'll be over in half an hour."

Sandy rolled her eyes. "Men - wanting to buy a plane before we have a place to put it."

When the owner arrived, Buff could barely hide his excitement. The plane looked brand new. Without even trying to negotiate a lower price, Buff bought the plane for $350,000. They shook hands and the previous owner left.

Buff shot Sandy a wide grin.

"Let's go shopping!" he said.

"What? Don't you consider spending $350 thousand enough shopping for one day?"

"Not even close. We need to outfit ourselves with winter gear," Buff said. They went to Rapid City's best store for outdoor winter gear. Buff found a clerk.

"I want Sandy here, to have 50° below zero rated mittens and 30° below zero rated gloves."

"I want us to have gear to go into very cold places such as mountains in the winter," Buff said and left Sandy and the clerk at the gloves display and found Arctic coveralls rated to 50° below zero for Sandy.

He found the clerk again and asked her to outfit him the same way. He found the hunting dog area and got Lucky several pairs of dog shoes.

Soon the pair had four large duffel bags stuffed with the gear. They put the duffel bags, ice axes and several hundred feet of rope in the airplane.

Buff had ads placed in publications all over the country. In two days, they got their first request to help from Cameron, Montana. Buff yelled for Sandy and told her they had their first job.

"I can be at the airport in thirty minutes," Sandy said excitedly.

"See you at the airport!" Buff answered.

John Stires, an AGF flight instructor, sat next to Buff. Buff was at the controls. He took to flying as though he had some bird in him. Sandy listened to the instructions John offered.

In flight, Sandy called the missing boys' parents and they said, "They are veteran ice cliff climbers. I just don't know what could have happened to them."

It was the middle of winter and the two boys had gone to climb ice cliffs. Sandy reassured them that their boys would be found, and called the Cameron Police. There were only three police officers and the chief in the department. Sandy asked him if they knew two boys were missing.

"Yes, we're aware, and I've known those boys since they were born. Who are you?"

"We've been called in to help find the boys. I'm Sandy. I was a lieutenant deputy sheriff until recently. Buff is on lead, and is a semi-retired sheriff and ex-Marine with extensive training. We have our dog Lucky, a Belgian Malinois, who is undoubtedly one of the best trained law enforcement and Search and Rescue dogs in the world."

"Please, come and help us as soon as possible. We'd really appreciate it," the chief said.

"We're in a private plane and expect to get to the scene in under an hour," Buff reported.

"We have had volunteers looking all over the cliffs where the boys were climbing. We have found nothing, and those boys can probably last only another day or so in that cold, even if they were prepared for the conditions," the police chief said.

"We'll be there as quickly as we can," Sandy assured the chief.

Two of the department's three SUV patrol cars were waiting at the small town's landing strip for Buff to land the plane. It was only his second try and he did it like a pro. One patrol car and officer took John to a small motel in Cameron.

Buff, Sandy, and the other officer worked fast to load their gear into his SUV. Lucky ran to the edge of the runway and went potty.

Buff whistled and Lucky hopped in the back of the SUV. The dog found his spot on top of their gear and laid down, looking out through the windshield.

"What's first?" the officer asked.

"Let's go by the boy's parent's house and pick up something of theirs that Lucky can get a scent from," Buff suggested.

It was only about ten minutes out of the way from their travel to the scene. "I want to start with the areas that the volunteers and your fellow officers haven't checked yet," Buff said.

"Right. I know there are many places left to search. We really appreciate your help."

They all piled out of the SUV. The chief of police and another officer met them while they were suiting up. Sandy was putting snow booties on Lucky's paws. Buff put the boys' dirty socks down from their parents' houses for Lucky to smell. Lucky and Buff lead the others out to the trail

They began calling Alan and Donny, the missing boys' names. They had walked a while when suddenly Lucky found the scent trail. He barked once and pulled hard on the leash. Even Buff had to brace himself.

Lucky took them on a three-mile quick hike through the rough territory. The older chief of police had to sit down and one officer stayed with him.

Lucky and his group found themselves about a hundred yards from an ice cliff and Lucky alerted again. Buff knew the boys were there, by Lucky's behavior. As they neared the ice cliff the boys heard them and called back, "Here! We're over here!"

Buff turned Lucky loose and he ran straight to the boys, licking their faces in turn. The boys groaned a bit from moving their injured limbs but were so grateful they praised Lucky. Lucky laid down next to them and waited for Buff and the others.

The chief ordered the town's only helicopter to act as a medevac to get the boys to the hospital in Great Falls and called the hospital to alert them of the injured coming in.

The hospital director told them that only one of their choppers was available. Buff agreed and said it was enough. The older Cameron chopper arrived first and they took the more severely injured boy on board. Soon after the chopper from Great falls arrived they loaded in the second boy.

A paramedic asked, "Who is in charge here?"

The chief pointed at Buff and Buff pointed at the chief. Buff said, "It doesn't matter."

"Well, whoever it was that did the first aid, did a great job," the paramedic said.

"Both boys had both legs broken, one had shoulder injuries and probably a broken arm. Sandy reported to the chief. "One boy, Donny, has a deep cut on his cheek that we bandaged."

"What happened?" the chief asked.

"Donny said they'd almost reached the top when Allen's ice ax slipped. Allen lost his grip and fell. Allen landed on Donny. Their ice anchor gave way and both fell to the bottom," Sandy explained.

On the way back to the airplane, an officer drove; so Sandy, Buff, and Lucky rested. "I'm so glad you started this business. We can do a lot of good," Sandy said.

"I think we can - all we have to do is our best," Buff agreed. Lucky yawned and put his head down.

It was Sandy's turn to fly the plane. She gave them a smooth flight with their instructor's help.

Almost three hours later they arrived in Rapid City. They went home and took showers first thing. Soon they were both sawing logs with Lucky guarding the foot of their bed.

The very next day they got a call from Hudson Wyoming. Two girls were missing. They had been missing for over 24 hours and the police expected foul play.

The Hudson runway was short, but Sandy had no problem landing safely. Two sheriff's patrol cars were waiting for them.

"I'm Sheriff Jim Coble and this is my Deputy Lee Peterson." Buff introduced himself, Sandy, and Lucky, and the humans shook hands.

"The girls that are missing are 15 years old," Sheriff Coble said.

"What have you got so far?" Buff asked.

"Because of the circumstances surrounding their disappearance, we suspect they were abducted."

"We'll need some of the girls' clothing or other belongings, such as a hairbrush for Lucky to get a scent to follow. Where do you suggest we start?"

"We have lots of summer cabins and a few abandoned ones that are in disrepair," the sheriff said.

"You drive," Buff said to Sheriff Coble. Buff and Lucky followed him to his car. Sandy got a ride from a Deputy to go to the girls' house to get some questions answered and pick up some things for Lucky to smell.

Buff, Sandy, and Lucky met up and went in the sheriff's car and the deputy's car to continue searching for clues. They spoke to each other using the radio.

"That last cabin we searched was empty too," Sandy said.

"Yeah, maybe we should focus on the cabins that are the farthest from the office and motor home parking," Buff suggested.

"Yeah, those abandoned cabins sound intriguing," Sandy agreed.

"Will do," the sheriff said and made a hard right onto a narrow dirt road. The road was slick in spots and the cars felt like they were floating in places. The deputy and sheriff handled the driving on snow and ice very well.

After three and a half hours they spotted a cabin ahead with smoke coming out of the chimney.

"Nobody should be here, that's one of the abandoned cabins," the sheriff told Buff. Buff called Sandy on the radio and told her.

They stopped both cars. Each driver backed their vehicle just off the road to be hidden by the terrain. They didn't want to be seen by anyone in the cabin.

All the people and the dog climbed silently out of the vehicles, being careful not to slam the car doors.

"I'll take Lucky around the perimeter to check for a scent trail. We'll be back. Wait here until we return with our report," Buff said. The others nodded in agreement.

On approaching the dilapidated cabin he decided to bring Lucky up close from the side that had blacked-out windows. It definitely looked like someone was hiding something. Lucky smelled the trail and when they got close, he sniffed all around the base of the walls. He even jumped up and sniffed the bottom edge of the windows. He growled softly and lay down at Buff's feet. Buff led Lucky back the way they came, jogging. He quickly reached the others.

"The girls are in there, and I think I'd like the front and back doors to be kicked in at the same time. Sheriff, would you and your deputies take the lead with your guns?"

"We'd be happy to," the sheriff agreed. His deputy nodded in agreement.

"I don't know why, but I have a bad feeling about this," Buff admitted, whispering to Sandy.

"You're with me Sandy, we'll take Lucky in the front door behind the deputy. He will bring any runners down," Buff said.

When Buff was sure everyone had time to get into place, he whistled. The sheriff and the deputy with Buff kicked in the doors. Buff and Sandy saw two naked girls with a man on top of each of them. Buff said, "Police, you're under arrest!"

"Go away and I'll let them go!" one man said. Without another word, the sheriff and deputy moved in, yanked the guys off, and roughly put them on the floor, their hands behind their backs.

Sandy ran forward to cover the girls with a blanket. They were screaming. One had her head buried in a pillow, the other had been trying futilely to climb over the head of the bed to get away. Sandy's soothing words helped them calm down.

The men were cuffed and dragged out of the cabin. The males all followed, leaving Sandy alone with the girls. The deputy jogged back to the vehicles to bring them forward one at a time. She got on the radio for an ambulance and crime lab team.

Sandy spoke nicely to the girls and asked if they felt pain anywhere. They both shook their heads no, but they looked very uncomfortable.

Sandy said, "An ambulance will be here soon to take you to be sure you are both okay. Do you want to call your parents to come?"

"Can't we just go home?" one girl asked.

"No, you may have been hurt, and to keep this guy in jail, they will examine you both for evidence that will hopefully put him away for a long time. I'm so sorry you have to go through all this, but it is necessary."

"Fine," said one girl.

The other said, "okay."

"Do you know where your clothes are?"

"Over there, I think," said one girl.

"That will be evidence as well. The ambulance will have scrubs you can wear - try not to worry."

She got another couple of blankets and wrapped them up individually so they could move around if they wanted to.

Lucky came back inside the cabin and gently licked one girl's hand, the other girl offered her hand too and they both smiled briefly.

The girl's parents, all four, met them at the hospital. They hugged their girls for a long time. Then they shook hands and hugged Lee, Jim, Sandy, and Buff.

Buff said, "This is the best part, right Sandy?"

"Sure is, I'm glad it turned out. I hope the girls receive all the help they need," Sandy said.

On all their flights, John kept instructing Buff and Sandy on how to be good pilots. When they weren't actually flying someplace. John scheduled time to practice with them. After each had performed an air move they would trade places for the other to do the same move.

Both quickly got the hang of flying. At the end of one lesson, John said, "I'm going to teach you how to land in crosswinds next."

The next lesson was there before they knew it. The winds were perfect for practice landing. It was Sandy's turn first at a landing at Rapid City Regional airport and she had a smooth landing.

Sandy pushed full throttle on the speed levers and they went around again for Buff to practice a landing. Buff's landing was a little rough, but they still had a couple of months to go to get certified as pilots.

Six months later, Buff and Sandy were licensed pilots. Buff had John give him some more training on GPS. Sandy asked Buff, "Can we take turns piloting?"

"Of course - I wouldn't have it any other way."

The next day they got a call from a Native American person who asked them if they could check an old Native American school site for unmarked graves in Nebraska.

The Native American gentleman said, "You're getting famous so I imagine you're too busy for us. I also don't think we can afford you."

"Does free sound good to you?" Buff said. "This kind of request is why we started this business. What is your name, sir?"

"I'm called Big Bear, and yes, I think free would work out just fine for us."

"I thought it might," Buff smiled.

"So you'll come?" Big Bear asked.

"We'll leave by six in the morning. Where is the nearest landing strip?" Buff asked.

"There is one close by. It's well-maintained too. All the farmers and ranchers seem to be flying planes now," Big Bear said.

The next morning Buff, Sandy, and Lucky took off for the site. It was their first time not having their instructor along. Buff flew first. Sandy said, "You only went first because you are bigger than I am."

They met up with Big Bear near the landing strip. Big Bear told them, "The school was called St. Mary's Indian Boarding School. I can take you right to the site. Our town nearby is called Whitman."

Ten other people showed up with Big Bear to help if needed. Big Bear said, "You can drive one of our SUVs with all of your equipment, your partner, and your dog."

Sandy drove the SUV while Buff looked at maps and searched the web on his phone to find out more about the area.

"Buff, get off your phone, we're here," Sandy said.

Buff replied, "Already?"

"It was only about four miles and mostly paved. I hope this will be an easy mission," Sandy said. Everyone got out of their vehicles and met near Big Bear's pickup truck. They all stood quietly for a moment, looking at the remains of the old boarding school.

"One of the ranchers uncovered the remains of a young child. We figured that there were probably more unmarked graves," Big Bear said, breaking the silence.

"Take us to where they found the child's remains, could you?" Buff asked.

They walked out to the back of the school grounds and a short way into a farmer's field. The area had been left undisturbed by the farm workers. Lucky sniffed around while the humans reflected on how awful the situation really was.

"How these kids must have suffered?" Sandy asked.

Just then, Lucky barked and took off. Running, only a short distance, he alerted again to a spot about fifteen feet from where the farmer found the first body. Buff said, "Dig here, carefully," and he pointed at the ground just in front of where Lucky had laid down.

It didn't take long to dig a large hole with all the help they had. About three feet down they found another skeleton.

"Have you been watching Lucky?" Sandy asked Buff.

"Yeah, and he's found another one already. Guys, over there is next." Buff and about half of the volunteers left the others to finish recovering the last body. They started digging again.

Buff leaned down and petted Lucky. "Thank you, you big beautiful mutt. At least these souls will be laid to rest properly even after all these years."

Sandy stayed with Lucky and after a few minutes' rest, she took him out in the field and gave him the "find" command.

Buff went back to the SUV that had all their stuff in it and laid out a grid, to make sure they checked the whole area. He marked where the bodies had already been found to see if there was any pattern to how the bodies had been buried. He heard Lucky bark once again and looked in time to see him lying down. He found that spot on his map and marked it while walking back to where they were working. He showed his map to Big Bear.

"This is good. It will help a lot," Big Bear said. After seven hours the map showed where Lucky had alerted to sixty-five bodies. Some of the volunteers were still filling the holes back in.

"DNA lasts in buried bones for 100-10,000 years. I hope you will be able to get a lot of the remains back to the families," Buff said.

A man walked up from the area where they had parked and stopped near Buff. "Hello, my name is Stands Alone. How can we ever repay you?"

"You don't have to repay us, but do like drumming, singing, and dancing from your tribe. Would that be okay?"

"Sure thing."

Stands Alone and one of the volunteers that had been digging went to the tribe and asked them if they could quickly get a celebration together. The tribal president said, "We'll have a Pow-wow for them in two to three hours. We'll also have plenty of food and drink ready."

Buff and Sandy sat together watching the dancers after eating a perfectly prepared buffalo roast with fry bread, watermelon, and corn. Lucky also got buffalo for his dinner.

"This pow-wow was the best! And you got it all together in such a short time. I hope there is such a thing as ghosts, so all the kids we found today could have been here," Buff said.

"We are very happy to do it for you," Stands Alone said.

"We're sorry but we've got to get going. We have a lot to do before we get another call - but we really appreciated and enjoyed the pow-wow," Sandy said.

"You're welcome, and thank you for recovering all those bodies for us. Here is some more buffalo for Lucky on the road," Big Bear said. "Each skeleton was put in separate body bags and we will contact several medical examiners to come here, as you instructed, Buff. Somehow the news reporters have already heard about this and will be here in the morning to get the story and take pictures. Are you sure you can't stay?"

"No, we can't, but let me know how it turns out," Buff said.

"Yes, and if there's anything else we can help you with, keep our number," Sandy said.

Big Bear petted Lucky before the dog loped off to catch up with his masters. Stands Alone followed them and helped load all their stuff back into the plane from the SUV. Sandy got in the pilot's seat and when she looked up, she saw about 150 Native Americans, many still in costume from the pow-wow, had shown up to send them off. They were waving and giving them thumbs-up gestures.

Everyone moved to the sides of the landing strip when Sandy started the plane's engine. They continued to wave until the plane was out of sight.

When they got home at about eight o'clock the phone was ringing. "Hello?" Buff said, tentatively.

"Hello, this is Sheriff Adams from Grandview Wyoming, and we have two missing boys. I called around and was told by several people that you might have the best-trained dog in the world and you are our best chance of finding the boys."

"Sure, how long have they been missing?" Buff asked.

"The boys have been missing for about 28 hours now. Any chance you can come and help us find them right away? It is cold up there in the foothills of the Big Horns."

"Yes, Sheriff Adams, can you be reached at this number?" Buff asked.

"Yes, hope to hear from you soon," said the sheriff.

"Are you up to going out again so soon?" Sandy said.

"Yes, I'm fine," Buff answered.

"If you're going, I'm going," Sandy said. "We better get ready. I need coffee."

"We will fill up our thermos on the way back to the plane," Buff said.

Buff called Sheriff Adams as they hit the road again with Sandy driving. "We're on our way. We'll need something belonging to the boys for the dog to get a scent from."

"Already obtained, sir," Adams said.

On arrival at the airstrip, Buff, Sandy, and Lucky were met by Sheriff Adams. They drove to the temporary command center that was set up for the search and was met by several deputies.

"Here are the clothes that we got from the boy's parents." Sheriff Adams handed Sandy a stuffed full plastic grocery bag. Lucky was already sniffing it and wagging his tail.

"The boys were last seen walking between two hills about two miles from here," Sheriff Adams said. "We'll take you to the site."

"Thanks, Sheriff," Buff said.

"You've done a great job. Can we leave now?"

"Sure thing, this SUV is for you and your team to use. My deputy already loaded all your gear from the patrol car into it."

Soon they were at the place where the boys were last seen. Buff let Lucky smell the clothes again before he let him out of the SUV. Lucky started sniffing the air, alerted right away and they set off between the two hills.

Hiking was very difficult for the humans, Lucky was having a great time jumping on top of boulders and dodging smaller rocks.

They had been hiking for almost three hours when Lucky alerted them to a small, ground-level crack in the side of a cliff.

The boys were in there and one said, "Grizzly!"

Buff couldn't hear him and told him to speak up.

The boy cried, "Grizzly!" nearly screaming.

Sandy, a few meters away screamed, "Bear!" Lucky charged the charging bear. He was charging right at Buff and the opening in the cliff where the boys hid.

Lucky jumped at the grizzly's throat. The bear took a swipe at Lucky and sent him flying 12 feet. Buff pulled his 44 magnum and shot at the grizzly when he was about 35 feet away. He hit him twice in the chest but it didn't even slow him down. When the bear was about ten feet away, he shot again, this time hitting the bear in the head. Sandy pulled her gun too and fired off eight rounds. The bear dropped at Buff's feet. Buff saw it was a female and was nursing cubs by the enlarged mammary glands. Buff fell to his knees, put his head on the grizzly's head and sobbed for several minutes.

Sandy went to the cliff and yelled inside.

"Are either of you hurt?"

"We're okay," came a voice from the cave.

"It's okay to come out," she said. "The bear can't hurt you."

When Buff stood up he ran to his dog who was slowly coming toward him, whining. Lucky was wearing his vest, but two of the bear's claws missed the vest sinking into Lucky's fur and skin. Lucky whined as Buff touched the area. Lucky had two deep cuts on his side and was bleeding.

Buff picked Lucky up carefully, but Lucky whined loudly.

"It's okay, I gotta get you back to the truck," Buff said soothingly. The boys started to follow Buff, but Sandy called them.

"If you boys are up to it, could you help me find that bear's cubs?"

"Sure!" the boys said excitedly.

Buff heard her, and stopped for a second, remembering how rough it had been to get there. He called Sheriff Adams using his mobile phone and requested a chopper.

"No, it doesn't have to be medical, and the boys were not injured. The chopper only has to be fast, Lucky was hurt by a charging bear trying to protect me, and there will probably be one or two bear cubs."

"Buff! We found the cubs! Where are you?" Sandy yelled. "There are two - come help us carry them. They aren't as small as I'd hoped."

She listened for a moment and didn't hear Buff answer.

"Buff! Where are you?" Sandy called again. "Hold on boys. I gotta go find him. I'll be right back, watch the cubs, but don't try to pick them up yet, okay?"

"Okay," both boys agreed.

Running back, Sandy spotted Buff. He was sitting on the trail about 50 feet from the dead bear's body. She ran up to him and saw he had Lucky lying across his lap.

"Oh no!" Sandy cried. "He's not?!"

"No, he's alive," Buff confirmed.

Lucky weakly moved his tail in greeting.

Sandy kneeled to pet Lucky's head and check on Buff.

"Are you hurt?" Sandy asked him.

"No, I'm fine, but there is no way we can walk back carrying Lucky and two bear cubs. I ordered a chopper and told them where we were."

"Oh, okay. That will be better since Lucky is hurt. You know he would die protecting you."

"You too, I'm sure. I'm so sad and sorry he got hurt!" Buff said with tears in his eyes. "I can't believe we killed a bear - let alone a female nursing cubs!"

"You had no choice, Buff."

Seeing that Buff was so upset made Sandy tear up too. For a couple of minutes, she hugged him from behind and squeezed his shoulders as she stood up. She jogged back to the boys who she found playing with one cub. The furry brown ball was on one of the boys' laps getting his ears scratched. The other one was feisty, growling when the other boy touched him, which he did over and over, giggling.

"Don't tease him!" Sandy yelled. "Leave him alone!"

The boy stopped messing with the grumpy bear cub and joined the other boy in petting the nice, calm cub.

Watching the boys with the cubs gave Sandy an idea. She found that her mobile phone had a signal and called the owner of Bear Territory.

"Hello, I'm a rescuer who is in the mountains right now. We came across two orphaned grizzly bear cubs because we had to shoot the mother. Would you be able to take the cubs in?"

"Of course, we always have room and we're set up to raise them right," the male voice said. "I also know the director of Woodland Park who we will send them to because they have lots of Grizzlies."

"Thank you so much! We're waiting on a rescue chopper now to get us and the bear cubs back to civilization. We have an injured dog we need to take to the vet first, then we'll bring the cubs to you. Do you have a helipad?"

"Not officially, but we have a cleared area that we use for one."

"Good, we can bring them straight to you then. I'll call when we are on the way," Sandy said. "We're near Loveland, Colorado right now; so it'll be a while."

A few minutes after Sandy was off the phone, she heard the helicopter in the distance. She looked around and saw it approaching.

"Okay boys, stay with the cubs - and don't tease them!" Sandy said as she went off to find Buff.

Buff was standing, still holding Lucky, and watching the chopper land in a mostly clear place nearby. As Buff took Lucky to where they landed, four-game and fish officers jumped out with cages for the cubs.

As she passed them, Sandy told them where the cubs were and pointed. She went to Buff to be sure Buff and Lucky were comfortable.

"How are you doing, Buff?" she asked.

"I'm okay. I think Lucky will be okay too. I think the cold helped stop the bleeding. Lucky is shivering though."

While the bear cubs were being caged and brought to the chopper, Sandy found the first aid kit under the chopper's seat. She got the gauze out and with Buff's help to lift the dog, she put a belly wrap on him. She put the silver emergency blanket around him too and tucked in the edges. Buff kindly held Lucky's paws under the blanket too.

They loaded the two cages in front of the cubby hole where Buff sat with Lucky. The sweet bear was the closest. Everybody piled in and found a place to sit. The boys that they rescued sat on top of the cub's cages.

In flight, Lucky stretched so that his nose could smell the cub's fur. The sweet cub put his nose to Lucky's nose for a sniff and a lick. Buff hoped that it meant that Lucky was already feeling better.

In the quiet town of Loveland, the chopper landed in a large, nearly empty parking lot. It was across the street from the local veterinary office. The vet had never had a patient come by helicopter before.

Buff got out, having never let go of Lucky and carried him across the street.

The helicopter took off again heading for Bear Territory to drop off the cubs. Sandy went with the cubs, and the chopper pilot kindly took her back out to the scene where Sheriff Adams was waiting.

They waited for the chopper to get far enough away that they could talk. "Did everything go smoothly?" Sheriff Adams asked.

"Yes. Buff is at the vet with Lucky and I haven't heard from Buff, but I'm sure Lucky will be fine too. The bear cubs are at Bear Territory. Do you have everything you need for your report?" Sandy asked.

"I do and have a good trip home. It'll be a long drive."

"I'm only driving as far as the plane, then I'll go meet up with Buff. I'm a licensed pilot too, you know?"

"I didn't, but I'm not surprised, and we'll pick up our SUV from the airstrip, then. Thank you very much - and tell Buff too."

"I will," Sandy said, and added, "I hope the next time we see you it's under better circumstances."

Sheriff Adams waved as she pulled out and headed for the plane. She got all their equipment loaded and started the plane's engine. She called ahead to Northern Colorado Regional Airport and filed a flight plan.

In no time she landed, and found her rental car was waiting for her.

She drove to Loveland and found the veterinary office. The vet greeted her himself in the office and took her back to where Buff was. He sat in the cage with Lucky, the door open, his legs hanging out waiting for Lucky to finish waking up from anesthesia.

"Well, how is he?" Sandy asked.

Buff looked up and grinned from ear to ear. "He's fine! Dr. Morton did surgery on him right away."

Dr. Morton spoke up, "Fortunately there was no organ damage. The claws did penetrate the abdominal wall but there was no organ damage. He took 40 stitches to close up the claw marks. I gave him fluids and I'll send him home with painkillers. You might want to use them tonight, I doubt he will need painkillers after that. If he's uncomfortable give him a dose as needed. The painkillers have side effects too and it's better not to give them for too long."

"I understand, Doc. When can we take him home?" Buff asked.

"As soon as he wakes up a little more. I understand you have a private plane to fly back to South Dakota. I know you're anxious to leave for home. Since you are a trained rescuer, Lucky can finish waking up on the plane if you'd like."

"Thank you so much Doctor. I hope we don't see you again, but it's good to know there is a good veterinarian in this area," Buff said.

"Is there any other care we can do for him?" Sandy asked.

"Well, you can take his stitches out after 10 days, no baths, no playing in the snow, no hard play at all until after the stitches come out, okay?"

"Okay, Doc. I'll make sure Buff and Lucky take it easy," Sandy promised.

The next two weeks were a vacation not only for Lucky, but for Buff and Sandy too.

One day, Buff gave Lucky the last of the buffalo meat that Big Bear gave him. The dog chomped it down as though he'd never been hurt. Buff watched the dog for a few moments and then he went to the kitchen to find out what he was having for lunch.

He saw his beautiful blonde wife at the cutting board on the counter. He went up to her quietly and hugged her from behind, slightly surprising her.

"You should not sneak up on me when I'm holding a knife," she said, teasing him.

Buff spoke softly in her ear, "I'm not scared."

He hugged her again, this time holding her arms, making her stop cutting the zucchini.

Buff said, "I'm so glad you're here. I'm so glad to be home. That was a rough one, for me anyway. I hated that we killed the bear."

"You've said that before honey. I hated it too, but it was unavoidable. Stop thinking about it now if you can," Sandy said. "How's your head?"

"It's fine - that nap did me a lot of good."

"I'm glad. It's unusual for you to complain about any discomfort. I was worried about you," Sandy said while trying to cut the zucchini.

Still standing behind Sandy, Buff gave her a tight squeeze. He put a line of light kisses up her arm and shoulder. Then slowly up her neck, giving her goosebumps. She purred softly and visibly relaxed.

He turned her around in his arms and kissed her on the lips lightly, teasing. She increased the pressure on his lips.

After a long kiss. They walked together out on the deck and sat on a porch swing. It started to rain, but they didn't go inside. They sat together, with their arms around each other and gazed into each other's eyes. They watched the rain for a short while, but it was long enough to get them soaked.

"The first rain of spring," Buff said after several minutes.

"Yeah, it's so warm and I'm hot," she grinned. Her fingers found the buttons on his shirt and she unbuttoned them slowly.

Looking up into his eyes she said, "I think I should have worn some…mmmm."

Buff's kiss cut her off mid-sentence. "Shhhh…" he hushed her softly.

Not that Sandy was trying to get away, but Buff tangled his fingers in her hair and held her close to his chest. He used her hair to guide her head as he kissed every inch of her face.

Excited, she just pulled on the last three buttons on his shirt and popped them off. While they kissed, she found his tight stomach and her fingers danced feeling his muscles and ribs. She lifted her face so he could kiss down her neck, collarbone, and anywhere else he wanted to kiss.

Sandy too, kissed lower. With her fingers, she rubbed and teased Buff's nipples.

"Wow-ee," Buff moaned and leaned back against the armrest on the porch swing. She ran her fingers back and forth across her husband's rain-soaked, hard abdominal muscles, his smooth strong flanks, and finally behind his back. Hugging him tightly, she worked his back muscles down to his butt with both hands.

Buff moaned and purred and kissed and sucked on Sandy until he thought his pleasure center would overload. Nuzzling her in her ear and behind her ear was driving her crazy with passion.

Finally more urgently, Sandy grabbed handfuls of Buff's rain-soaked hair. She pressed her lips to his, exploring his entire mouth, even counting his teeth with her tongue. Finally, she ended the kiss but stayed nose-to-nose with him.

He said, "You are so beautiful Sandy - I can't believe how lucky I am to have you as my own."

"I think I'm pretty lucky too."

Sandy slowly got off of Buff and stood up straight. He thought she was just repositioning, for some more fun, but she said, "I gotta go finish lunch. Come with me - you can get the meat ready to grill," giggling as she skipped away.

"AAhh!" Buff cried. "You are such a tease!" He reluctantly got up and followed her back to the kitchen.

Three uneventful days later, Lucky greeted Buff enthusiastically when he came out after a well-deserved nap. He rubbed his head while he thought about how his headaches were coming more often and more intensely.

"Hey boy, you're looking great!" Buff stopped to pet Lucky and gave him a big hug.

He found Sandy watching TV. She grabbed the remote off of the coffee table and turned off the TV when she saw him approaching.

"How was your nap? Do you feel better?" Sandy fired questions at him.

"I do, physically." Buff began. "I feel like I need to do a sweat, vision quest, or Yuwipi and maybe even a sun dance to purify."

"Of course, I'll help you do whatever you need to do to feel better. Do you want me to call Charles?"

"No, I'll get a glass of water and call him myself - thanks though." Buff smiled at his wife. "Did you already give Lucky his antibiotics for tonight?"

"No, I plan to give them to him with his dinner," Sandy said.

"Oh right, I forgot he should have that prescription with food," Buff said. "My brain really feels like mush." He got his water and went to his office to make the call.

Sandy went to play with Lucky. He still had his stitches in after his surgery so they had to be gentle. She got his chewy toy and they rolled around, gently on the rug playing with the toy together.

In his office, Buff called Charles, a Lakota Medicine man who he had become good friends with. He asked if he would hold a sweat lodge to heal his migraines.

"Of course. I'd love to do this for you. You're a very sacred man. Let's have a sweat tomorrow to get started."

"Would you let me do the vision quest at Bear Butte?"

"Yes, I'll arrange it," Charles agreed. "Anything else we can do?"

"I would like to be part of a Yuwipi and Sundance too. I have taken some time off and want to spend it healing if I can."

"What's wrong?" Charles asked.

"I feel depressed and now I'm having headaches," Buff admitted.

The next morning Buff got up, fed Lucky and gave him his antibiotic pills. Sandy went to the kitchen and made human breakfast for herself and Buff. They talked about utilitarian things, like the weather, cleaning up the kitchen, and doing dishes. Then Buff left the house. He went out to where his mother's cremation ceremony had taken place.

"This is just how she wanted it," he said out loud. "Already, I have to look hard to see any trace that it happened here."

He remembered everything like it was only the day before and walked over to where her bones had been buried. He sat on the ground near her bones and meditated.

Sandy watched a little TV but grew restless because Buff had not come home. She read, cleaned the kitchen and vacuumed. She ordered fence posts for the front drive entrance to the house. When she realized that it had been over four hours since he'd left. She got up from the office chair to go find him. She was elated when she looked outside and she saw him walking toward her.

"Are you okay?"

"Yeah, but it's time. I have to leave to go to the sweat. Are you coming?"

"I think I'll stay here with Lucky. I don't want to be a distraction for you."

"Okay. I'll be back as soon as it's over. Don't wait up," Buff said. He planted a warm kiss on her lips, and again on her cheek. He held onto her hands until the last second as he moved away. He only let go of her when he had to.

At the site of the sweat lodge, Charles greeted Buff, smiling. He said, "The lava rocks are ready. Your timing is perfect."

"Good," Buff said simply.

"The rocks have been in the fire for five hours. We're going to be using 36 rocks. We will use nine rocks at each door and it's really going to be hot in there. Try not to leave the sweat."

"There's no way I'd leave," Buff said. "I appreciate you getting this set up so fast."

"There will be four other people with us," Charles said. "And I'm going to call in the lightning beings."

"The weather report said there was no chance of rain," Buff said.

"Oh ye of little faith," Charles said, and Buff smiled a weak smile.

Everyone present moved toward the sweat lodge including Buff and Charles. As everyone chose their place inside, the fireman, who was appointed to bring in the hot rocks, started his duties. He placed nine rocks in the hole in the center of the lodge.

Charles closed the door, which was no more than a tent flap. Before sitting down, Charles poured several ladles of water over the rocks. The temperature inside the lodge got very hot and humid very fast.

The other people in attendance, Danny Two Bulls, Steve Many Horses, Debra Cougar, and Randy Lone Eagle prayed in turn. Danny spoke first.

"Grandfather, please give my family a long and healthy life. Please let my grandmother go down the road peacefully, help Buff get rid of his migraines and keep him strong in his work. Metakuye Oyiasin."

"Please keep my family safe and well. Please keep me on the red road. Heal Buff of his migraines. Thank you for caring for me. Please help the Lakota people. Please help us in ending the meth crisis on the rez," Steve prayed.

Debra prayed next. "Please guide and protect us all. Please help my grandmother with her Alzheimer's and please heal Buff," she finished.

In the distance, thunder rumbled long and low. Buff got chill bumps even in the heat of the sweat lodge and was more sure of his healing.

Randy Lone Eagle began to pray as though he didn't notice the thunder. "Grandfather, please help us all stay well and on your path. Please cure Buff of his migraines so he can keep doing his good work."

The thunder grew louder and sounded closer.

Finally, Buff prayed, "Please watch over everybody and keep us in your good graces. Grandfather Wakan Tanka, Tunkashila, please keep us healthy and protect us. Please watch over and protect Sandy and Lucky."

The other people in the sweat prayed in Lakota.

A drummer started drumming and everybody took part in singing healing and sacred songs. They sang for 20 more minutes and then Charles said, "Open the door."

Someone stood and opened the tent flap. Buff tried to get as close as he could get to the door and laid on the ground on his back. He felt a little breeze.

The fireman brought in nine more red-glowing lava rocks and placed them in the hole. Charles said, "Close the door." He ladled several more cups of water over the rocks. Steam filled the lodge, and thunder sounded closer.

Buff thought to himself, "I'm amazed that this medicine man can call in lightning spirits."

The lodge was hotter than it had been after the rocks were brought in through the second door. The group prayed, sang, and chanted for about 35 minutes. Charles said, "Open the door."

The door was opened and the fireman brought in nine more rocks. Once the rocks were in the pit, the door was closed. Thunder clapped over and over very close by.

The group began to pray again, they sang and chanted to the Great Spirit. The wind was picking up and the thunder clapped and sounded like it was right over the lodge.

During the third door, and after nine more rocks were placed in the pit, they resumed praying and singing, but soon after they started again, Danny and Randy cried out "Metakuye Oyiasin," and they left the sweat. They just couldn't take the heat. There was no shame in leaving a sweat early if the heat is too much for you.

Another 30 minutes passed by and the fireman brought in nine glowing rocks. Charles added water for the last time. Buff wondered if he could continue to take the heat. He braced himself and decided to stay through the fourth door if it killed him.

As they started praying, singing, and chanting again, a huge wind came up. Buff was distracted and thought it must have been seventy miles an hour.

The flap blew open and two glowing orbs of blue light with a yellow fringe came inside. They were the spirits called by the medicine man. They were joined by a green, glowing orb that settled on Buff's head. Lightning flashed all around. After ten minutes or so the spirits left the lodge.

Charles got behind Buff and placed his hands on Buff's head. He said quiet prayers. When finished he called more loudly, "Open the door."

Everyone came out and Buff felt like he had been reborn. "That was the hottest sweat I've ever been in," Charles said. "I believe you're healed, Buff."

Buff grinned. Right then, nothing on his body hurt. He didn't know it then, but he would never have a migraine again in his life.

"Thank you so much, Charles. I know this takes a lot out of you, and I really appreciate it," Buff said.

"You are welcome," Charles said. "Let's put you on Bear Butte the day after tomorrow for your Hanbleceya."

"Right. I look forward to the vision quest."

Once he got home, Buff tried to creep into the house quietly so he wouldn't wake Sandy. He thought he'd made it until he tried to kiss her forehead without waking her. Her eyes popped open and she asked, "How did it go?"

"It was amazing," Buff said. "I'll tell you more in the morning."

"Okay," Sandy whispered

Lucky jumped up on the bed and laid down in a tight ball behind Buff's knees.

Buff and Sandy spent the next day resting, and Buff told her about the sweat. Her eyes were as big as saucers when he finished. "Really, you really saw spirits?"

"Yes, and I think I'm completely healed."

"Wow, that is amazing. I hope I can go to the next one with you."

"You sure can," Buff promised.

Buff and Charles did a sweat before daylight. Then they started their hike to the top of the mountain. When they reached the top, Charles, the medicine man smoked kinnikinnick with Buff. "Medicine men only smoke with people on the mountain they consider holy." Buff smiled shyly.

When they were done, Charles stood up and said, "I'll see you in three or four days. In the meantime, I'll know how you're doing up there, don't worry."

When Charles got back down to his vehicle, his mobile phone was ringing. He hurried and answered when he saw it was Sandy.

"Hello," she said. "I hope you don't mind my calling, but Buff didn't say much before he left, except that he'd be gone for several days."

"It's my pleasure. I'm glad you called. Buff is doing what we call a Hanbleceya, or vision quest. It provides spiritual power, social standing, bravery, and life's purpose. The first day on the mountain is brutal. Buff will only have his pipe. He will smoke his pipe a few times a day. At night he probably won't sleep much due to the cold. He will pray constantly."

"Oh poor Buff," Sandy cried.

"No, this is a good thing. He will come through it just fine. On the second day on the mountain, the temperature will be close to a hundred degrees in the daytime."

"Wow, thank you Charles for explaining," Sandy said before the call ended.

On top of the mountain, Buff thought his mouth was so dry he couldn't spit, so he tried to spit and he was right, he couldn't spit at all. He prayed and prayed, often praying out loud.

"Grandfather, please give me a vision to take back to the tribe. Please give me strength and health so I can keep helping people." Again, he was too chilled at night to sleep.

On the third day, he saw an eagle high above him. The eagle flew down and landed on a dead tree just fifty feet from where he sat. A bald eagle was a very good sign. He thought he had started hallucinating when a large coyote came within ten feet of him and lay down. The coyote just stared at him. He remembered that some other vision seekers saw a coyote and it gave them a vision.

On the fourth day, the coyote returned. It came into Buff's mind that he'd be of great benefit to his tribe if he had a vision. He had a vision and wrote it down in his notebook.

Just as he was thinking that he was dying of thirst, Charles showed up with a gallon of water. Buff greedily emptied it down in one go. They shared Charles' sacred pipe and smoked some more.

"Well, tell me, did you have a vision?" Charles asked.

"I think so," Buff said and spoke about his experience. He told Charles about the Eagle and the Coyote.

Charles said, "The Eagle represents what is highest, bravest, strongest, and holiest. That represents you. The coyote's message is to tell you and the tribe that you were born to help them."

"I understand," Buff said.

"We'll talk more about this, but let's go for now. I've planned the Yuwipi for Saturday night. Bring food to share before the ceremony."

"Will do," Buff said.

He got home dirty and worn out. Sandy offered to shower with him, but he was too tired even for that. He drank another gallon of water and took a quick shower. He lay on the couch. Sandy picked up his feet, only with his help, and sat down with his feet in her lap.

"Did you see what you hoped for?"

"I think so. I'll tell you about it when I'm not so tired."

"It's fine, Charles told me all about it."

"Really, when?"

"I called him to see what it was all about. What's next?"

"The Yuwipi will be on Saturday night."

"Okay, what is that? Can I go?"

"You can go, I'd like it and we need to bring food to share."

"I'll be glad to prepare something great to bring."

Saturday night came quickly. Buff and Sandy showed up with fry bread, a buffalo roast, and a big burlap bag of apples and oranges. Charles and Buff had a nice conversation before the ceremony began.

"Let's get started," Charles, the medicine man, said.

Buff and Sandy followed him into a large room with blackout blankets over the windows. All the participants sat on the floor in a large circle. There must have been about 60 of them. They all sat cross-legged.

Charles sat on the floor on a small, low stage. There was about one hundred feet of rope coiled neatly nearby and a very thick blanket lying next to him. Two large Lakota men wrapped the blanket very tightly around Charles. Then they began wrapping the rope very tightly around him from head to foot. That included his folded legs and his hands and even his fingers.

The lights were turned off and within seconds a spirit elk tramped all around the circle coming within inches of the participant's feet. The floor shook with the power of his hooves pounding on the floor in the circle.

Then a spirit warrior came in with bells and a bone whistle. He danced inches from the participants blowing the whistle. He wound up in the center of the circle and disappeared. In his place, an Eagle spirit flew up within inches of Buff's face. It hovered there for a full minute and then was gone too.

Next, a hand came out of the darkness and gently stroked the bottom of Buff's left foot. Buff had pain when he walked in that exact spot for quite a long time, but he never mentioned it.

Charles told the staff members to turn on the lights. He was sitting there with the blanket perfectly folded next to him and the rope perfectly coiled again as though it had never been used.

Buff thought, that would be impossible to do with no light. Buff looked at Sandy, who sat next to him. It was like she was in a trance.

He touched her shoulder. She slowly turned toward her husband. "That was ... was amazing! I saw everything - how did they do that?" Sandy whispered.

"Let's go home," Buff said. He took her hand and they walked back to their vehicle.

The next morning, Buff went outside to meditate again near his mother's bones. Sandy took Lucky to a veterinarian for a recheck appointment. Lucky was doing just fine but the vet didn't want to take the stitches out. He said to wait a few more days.

The next couple of days were uneventful, except when Sandy heard Buff call a podiatrist's office to make an appointment for the next day. She'd never heard him talk about foot pain or any issues with his feet.

She gave him space thinking he'd tell her when he thought it was time. Perhaps after the appointment.

Buff took an instant liking to the podiatrist, Dr. Martin. They had a nice conversation while the doctor examined Buff's feet.

The doctor stood up and announced, "You have a Morton's Neuroma. I'll have to cut out a nerve." Buff okayed the surgery and a few days later he was scheduled to have the procedure.

Sandy took Buff to his surgery appointment since he would not be allowed to drive after the surgery.

Sandy was sitting next to Buff's bed when he woke up.

"Hi, are you awake?" Sandy asked just to make sure.

"Yes, I think so. I'd really like to lay here another couple of days. But I gotta get back to work."

"We're just waiting for your discharge papers. The nurse said she'd come back in to help you get ready to go, and give you aftercare instructions," Sandy said.

The nurse told him he'd have to be off for another two weeks. That nearly infuriated him. Buff remained calm when he said, "Two weeks? I wanted to go back to work in a couple of days!"

"You can try, but I'm sure you will find it too painful to walk. If you damage your foot, we will have to repeat the surgery, and then you'll have to be off for another two weeks or more," said the nurse.

Buff crossed his arms on his chest and huffed like a little kid.

"Come on Buff," Sandy said. "Let's go home."

Buff and Sandy got home. Buff went to talk to Lucky about his surgery. The dog didn't seem to care at all, only chewing on his rubber bone. Sandy made dinner and they had a quiet evening.

Buff told Sandy when he was going to do his Sundance.

"But Buff, it's summer, it's not a great time of the year to do a Sundance. Your health is not the greatest right now and you told me about what goes on at a Sundance ritual," Sandy said.

"I'm fine. I'm working out again, my foot feels fine, no headaches or aches anywhere in my body. Are you coming with me?"

"No … well maybe. Lucky and I will tag along, in my vehicle in case you need anything."

"I won't, but you might find it interesting."

"I probably will, because I'm open to new experiences." Sandy forced a smile.

Sandy went to her first sweat lodge. The participants had to sweat before the Sundance. They all prayed for strength to get through the sacred ceremony. Sandy prayed that Buff would be okay.

After the sweat, Charles pulled Buff and Sandy aside and said, "The Sundance is a ceremony where people come together to heal and bring renewal to the people and the land. It is a prayer for life. The piercings will really hurt - even more than pulling your flesh and skin free. You will feel like quitting, Buff. Don't. You'll feel wonderful for a long time after the Sundance.

Sandy, you can dance on the outside of the circle."

"I understand," Sandy said. "I'm not sure I understand all of it, but I'm sure I will when it's all over."

Buff hugged Sandy and sent her off so he could prepare.

There were rocks to be cleared and a tall cottonwood pole to be stood up. When they cut the cottonwood pole, they do not allow any part of the cottonwood to touch the ground. The holy men cut off the branches of the tree and slipped the cottonwood into the six foot hole they had dug. There were large skulls from buffalo to arrange. There were many leather straps attached to the pole and bundles of skulls.

In the morning, the dancers started to dance in a shuffle. They would be doing this for 14 hours a day with only very short breaks if needed. Only after that time would they go back to their teepee.

When the long dance was finished and each man was near exhausted, it was time to do the piercing.

Buff went up to Charles when it was his turn. He found it easy to relax after dancing.

Charles, the medicine man, pierced Buff's chest skin with a bone knife. Buff gritted his teeth and softly moaned each time. The medicine man made four holes in Buff's skin.

Buff could barely hold still when Charles slid wooden pegs through the slits in his skin and flesh, but he did it, as all the men had done. Then Buff was led to the pole that already had long, leather thongs tied at the top. The end of the straps were tied to the wooden pegs anchored in Buff's and the other men's skin.

Among the participants there was a 15-year-old Lakota boy who chose to have his back pierced instead of his chest.

Buff found himself watching that young man as he was readied by the medicine man. The boy was to pull 12 buffalo skulls attached to the pegs in his back, until he got free.

Buff danced around the pole with the others. A few times he felt dizziness trying to creep up on him. He pushed it away and kept dancing. They danced around the pole, and the teen dragged the skulls for hours.

One by one the dancers at the pole started to lean back, trying to pull free. Buff also pulled against the straps tying him to the pole.

The young man dragging the skulls pulled the skulls through bushes and over rocks hoping they would get stuck and he could pull free. The problem was there were no large bushes or rocks big enough to really help him pull free all in one yank. A group of holy men surrounded the boy and danced, drummed, and sang to give the boy encouragement to keep trying.

Watching, Sandy winced when she saw them trying to pull free. She buried her face in Lucky's fur.

The dancers tied to the pole one by one, tore their flesh free from the pole. Buff gritted his teeth and gave it one good yank. He thought it would hurt a lot more than it did. When he was free he joined the others at a large teepee to get medical attention for their wounds.

The boy was the last to tear himself free. One of the holy men stood on a skull to help him by providing more resistance; so he could pull free. He finally pulled free and also went to the tent to get his wounds treated. The boy couldn't stop smiling at his success. He was now considered a man by the tribe.

After it was over, Charles, the medicine man, met with Buff to talk.

"You are now considered a Holy Man by the tribe. I know that you've had to kill men but you only did it as a last resort as a deputy and in the military for self-defense or the defense of others."

"Yes, I was hoping you'd say something like that," Buff admitted.

"Buff, your job is important, very important to many people. Keep it up!"

"Thank you so much, Charles, for your guidance and help. Here…" Buff handed Charles an envelope. "I'm giving you $700,000 to do with as you see fit."

Charles started to object, but Buff interrupted him.

"This isn't payment for the Sundance. I know you won't accept payment for the privilege. I'm sure you'll figure out a way to make some people's lives better."

Buff and Sandy were still sawing logs when Buff's mobile phone rang in the wee hours of the morning.

"Hello?" Buff groaned.

"Buff! This is Harold. Please, you've got to help me." Buff's old friend said excitedly.

"What's happening, Harold?" Buff moved to a sitting position on the bed.

"My elderly West Highland Terrier, Duke, has gone missing! Oh, God! He didn't come in last night from going potty. He didn't even get to eat last night! Buff, you have to help - that dog means the world to me!"

'Take it easy, Harold. I'll be at your place within an hour if we don't get any calls for rescue," Buff said and hung up the phone.

"I wanna sleep!" Sandy whined.

"Sleep dear. I don't think I'll need you on this one," Buff said, as he was getting Lucky ready to go, complete with a bulletproof vest.

Buff drove to Harold's place with Lucky in the front seat. It was barely dawn when he arrived. He found his friend pacing nervously in the front yard waiting for him.

"Let's get Lucky a scent of your dog, Duke, and then we'll go find him," Buff said as he got out of his Bronco.

Harold ran inside and brought out his dog's bed.

Lucky sniffed at it for nearly a full minute.

"Are you sure you're ready to go with me, Herold? It might be a long walk," Buff cautioned his older friend.

"Hell yes, I'm ready to go! We've got to find Duke! I have to be there when you find him, I'm sure he'll be scared."

Lucky started moving toward the trees at the edge of the forest, behind the houses. The two men followed Lucky and after about an hour, they found the Westie. The little dog whined when he saw people and when he tried to go to his master, he screamed like he was being killed. Buff jogged up to Duke and found that the dog's back paw was caught in a large clawed metal bear trap. Buff easily pried the trap off of the small dog's paw.

The excited dog ran three-legged to his owner. When the owner saw his paw, he sat down where he was and cried, "Oh God, Oh God - just look at his paw! It's mangled. Poor - Poor - Duke!"

"Calm down, it might not be as bad as it looks - either way, we have to get him to the vet."

Buff picked the 16-pound dog up to carry him back to the vehicles. Harold was so upset he had trouble keeping up with Buff. Finally, he cried, "Just take him Buff - Just run with him. Take him to the vet on Second Street. It's close and they know Duke."

"They won't be open yet," Buff stated, remembering how early it was.

"They handle emergencies too. There's a pager number on the door, the doctor will be there in five minutes after you page him. I'll be there as soon as I can."

"Alright, but wait for me to come back to get you. You shouldn't drive. I'll come back for you as soon as I hand him off to the doctor."

Harold reluctantly agreed. With the plans made, the older man sat down on a dead tree to catch his breath. Buff ran with the dog in his arms all the way to his vehicle.

The little dog was handed off to the vet as soon as the vet got there. Then Buff hurried back to Harold's house. He was afraid if his friend got back to his house before Buff got back that he wouldn't wait and try to drive. In his state of mind, that was bad.

Luckily Buff got there before Harold left, but it was close. He drove him back to the vet, and Harold never stopped talking.

"You know it's our damn governor doing this. She wants to trap all the state's critters so they don't eat any more pheasant eggs or chicks," Harold complained. "Doesn't she know that the world needs diversity?!"

Buff nodded, still driving. He thought about how much he would have liked Sandy to come after all. At least she could have talked to Harold. She was good at calming people down. She had calmed the pants off of him many times. He chucked to himself at that thought. In the meantime, Harold was still talking.

"Hasn't the governor heard about the Sixth Great Extinction Event? In trying to protect the pheasants other animals will go extinct! Not to mention pets that get trapped in those infernal traps!" Harold said.

When Buff and Harold got back to the vet, two technicians had arrived to help the vet and he had the dog in surgery. One of the techs came out to talk to Harold.

"You'll be happy to know that he won't lose his paw. The doctor is stitching him up."

"What about after surgery?! Will he be okay?"

Harold stammered. "Can I see him?"

"Not until his surgery is finished and he wakes up at least a little. I suggest you go someplace for breakfast and maybe some window shopping."

"Duke will have a thick bandage on his paw that will have to be changed and his foot checked every other day at first to be sure there is no swelling. He will be on antibiotics for ten days."

"Okay - Thank God we found him!" Harold backed up and sat in the waiting room where Lucky was on his "stay" command.

Buff took Herald to breakfast near the vet's office and spent a couple of hours with him until he could take him home with his dog.

Only a few days later, as Buff, Sandy, and Lucky were cruising down Omaha street, they got a call from dispatch who said that a woman was being assaulted in the President's Bar, just a couple of miles down the road. They got there in four minutes. They entered the bar and Buff saw a man strangling a woman. He had her feet off the ground. Buff went behind the big man and put his hands around the guy's neck. He lifted him off the floor, and the man let go of his victim.

Buff lowered the attacker slowly to the floor like he was merely lifting weights. The guy struggled weekly. The guy's face turned blue. Buff looked at his choked man and asked the man, "You want to take me on?"

"God no way!" the man said.

"So a big man like you only hurts women. I see. You coward," Sandy said as she put the cuffs on him.

"I wasn't going to kill her!"

"Did you think you were just dancing with her?" Buff said. "She was nearly dead when we got here. If we'd gotten here a minute later, she would have died."

Sandy read the man his rights and took him to the car. An ambulance showed up and the paramedics took care of his victim. She agreed to come later to the station to give her report.

Sandy and Buff took the perp to jail in their car. He eventually gotten years at the Sioux falls prison.

Buff hated men who abused women especially, and the sentence for the crime seemed much too lenient to him.

Buff got a call from Rapid City's Police Chief Koenig. The chief said, "We believe we have another meth lab North of Rapid city and they are adding Fentanyl to the opioids. We have five deaths directly related to the operation so far. Can you and your dog sniff out fentanyl?"

"Yes. He has to wear a K-9 mask air filter, which I just got him," Buff said. "If Lucky were to inhale some fentanyl he'd be dead in minutes."

"Thanks, Buff," Chief Koenig said. "How close does he have to be?"

"Lucky can be as far away as 16 miles if the wind is just right."

"No way!" Koenig said.

Buff said, "Way."

A couple of nights later, they took Lucky downwind to within a couple of hundred yards from the lab. Lucky sniffed the air and alerted. He lay down waiting for orders.

"Well, there are opioids there," Buff said. "What do you want to do?"

"We have to shut them down," Koenig said.

"How about ten lawmen and seven dogs, and the S.W.A.T. team?" Buff said.

"That sounds about right," Koenig agreed.

"Well, there are probably a lot of drugs in there," he said to the ten lawmen that were waiting for a report on the situation.

"Spread out in the forest and don't shoot anyone unless you have to."

Buff rode in the S.W.A.T. team's armored truck. After the ten lawmen had taken their places, Buff had the driver drive to the front door. Over the loudspeaker, Buff said, "You are surrounded by twenty cops. Come out with your hands on your heads." Buff heard something from the back of the lab.

Four men started running out of the back door and the highway patrol let their dogs loose. Buff heard the four men screaming their lungs out. The dog handlers got to the men and told their dogs to release and guard the men on the ground. They were all cuffed with zip ties. The officers locked the four men in their patrol cars. They cuffed their hands and attached them to the floor bolt.

One of the S.W.A.T. team members said, "I'm going inside." Before Buff could get a word out, the man was in the lab. A man hiding behind a barrel shot the S.W.A.T. team member and he dropped his AR-15. The bulletproof vest did its job but the S.W.A.T. team member fell over and he would be sore for quite a while.

"Come out with your hands up," Buff said. "You have one last chance."

The men shot out of the windows on all four sides of the lab. The lawmen all opened up and there was a terrible explosion. All four walls fell outward. Buff thought I guess there goes our evidence.

A few of the officers were shaken up and some even caught some flying debris from the explosion. By then an ambulance had arrived and the paramedics checked out all the officers. They then went to the four men locked in the cars and poured the antibacterial liquid into all their dog bite wounds. It must have been painful for all the screaming Buff heard.

They first took the men to the hospital for treatment and then took the four men to jail and charged them with the manufacture and distribution of controlled substances.

"I've got to go," Buff said. "I volunteered to help police the Sturgis Motorcycle Rally for the last two days of the event."

The next morning, Buff was at the rally with Lucky as promised. He had a fentanyl mask in his pocket just in case they ran into any possible Fentanyl labs.

It was a quiet morning with just a couple of DWI arrests. He and his dog were making their way between some parked bikes. Buff saw a staggering drunk a few yards down the sidewalk near the end of the row of bikes. He was fumbling with his keys, just about to get on a bike and drive away. The bike he stood beside was facing the road.

Buff got to the biker just as he sat down on the seat and started the bike. Buff simply picked up the back of the Harley so the back wheel was not touching the ground. The guy kept revving the engine wondering why he wasn't going anywhere. Buff dropped the motorcycle and the Harley tire dug into the pavement. The bike shot forward a couple of feet and went over with the rider still on the seat. Buff grabbed the guy by his leather jacket's collar so that his head would not hit the pavement.

He waited for a deputy sheriff to go by and waved him down. Buff asked him if he'd go book him and put him in a jail cell. The deputy had been slowly driving by and said, "I was looking for something to do."

Buff wandered down the street and went into a bar. A biker saw him and said, "Well you're a big drink of water."

"I've heard it before," Buff said. "I hope I never hear it again."

As they spoke, two local bikers got into a fight at the end of the bar. Buff groaned and yelled, "Stop - police!"

No one paid any attention to Buff. More and more bikers joined in the fight. One biker grabbed a guy around his neck and was strangling him to death. Buff roundhouse kicked the biker in his head, and he went down, lights out. The guy he was choking fell across the bar.

The fight kept going even though a couple of other law enforcement officers had come into the bar. Buff saw it was a single story building with no attic space on his way in, so he pulled his 44 magnum, put in his earplugs and put a shot through the roof. Everyone in the bar froze.

Nobody could hear anything for a while as their ears rang from the concussion. Buff started yelling as loudly as he could, taking out his own earplugs. "You take your gang to that wall," he said. "Stand with your backs to the wall." By that time the place was packed with law enforcement. Buff had highway patrol, police, marshalls, and more deputy sheriffs backing him up.

Buff asked a deputy Ssheriff friend, Donny Snortland to take the guy who had been choking the biker to death to jail and charge him with attempted murder.

"Great," Donny said.

Buff said to both gangs, "All of you guys check out of your motels or put away your tents. Get out of town and pray I don't see you here again." The gangs took turns walking out of the bar.

"Okay guys and girls, some of you follow them around until they leave town. Arrest them if they break the law in the least way. You'll probably have to arrest some of them for driving while intoxicated and it's not even noon yet," Buff said.

After Buff got home, he got a telephone call on his landline. A female said, "There was an 8.5 earthquake along the San Andreas fault. From the epicenter there is damage for over fifty miles in each direction. Near the fault, we have blocks and blocks of businesses and homes reduced to rubble. We need you and your dog here as soon as humanly possible to find the living and the dead. Will you be able to come?"

"Yes. We'll mobilize right now," Buff said. He called Sandy and she said she'd be ready in twenty minutes. He called the airport and asked them to be sure his Beechcraft had a full tank of gas and was flight ready. He called the sheriff and told him he didn't know how long he'd be gone.

Sheriff Carlyle said, "Thanks for letting me know."

Buff met Sandy at the airport. Sandy refilled the emergency aid packs while she waited for him. When they got to Los Angeles, Buff, Sandy and Lucky reported to the new headquarters building where they asked a few questions. The head of the rescue event said, "Thank you so much for coming. We'll get you to the worst of the damaged areas. I have a four wheel drive, all terrain, 4x4 vehicle that is yours to use. Take this radio with you and tell me what you need as you go."

While he was briefed, Buff put booties on Lucky's feet, then loaded their stuff from the plane to the ATV and left. They drove the ATV over land for many miles to the site of the worst damage.

They arrived at the coordinates and went to work.

Lucky alerted on a pile of concrete slabs.

"I'm going to lift this middle slab," Buff said. Buff lifted the 500 pound slab. They found four teens and only one had a few small abrasions. It was amazing that they'd escaped without serious injury.

Buff lifted each teen out, and Sandy gave them an ATV tour to the large triage tent set up in the area. The teens found their parents already at the tent.

Lucky alerted on the way to another collapsed building, and Buff could tell that Lucky was acting as if this was a cadaver site. They got a backhoe and moved rubble until they found a dead woman and dead man. They found IDs on both bodies. They were an elderly couple who had died instantly. Two volunteers put the couple in body bags.

"This is the most difficult case I've ever been on," Buff mumbled sadly to Lucky during a short water break. A highway patrolman ran up to Buff.

"There are live people in a collapsed building about a quarter mile from where we are." Buff, Sandy and Lucky followed the highway patrolmen to the new location.

"Anyone in there?" Buff yelled.

He heard several cries for help, and a very loud, deep voice said, "There are 14 of us in the basement."

"We'll get you out," Buff answered. He called for a backhoe.

After the backhoe arrived and started moving the large debris, Buff recognized the building and said, "My God, this is a school."

Soon the backhoe pulled all the concrete, brick, and debris off the first floor. Buff and others searched for a way to get to the basement. They found a staircase half full of concrete debris. Buff went down in the stairwell first and started handing up medium sized concrete slabs. Most of the slabs took two or three additional men to carry them away. Buff had some small cuts on his belly and chest.

When the stairwell was passable, the boys and girls below cheered. After they were out, they went around thanking all the rescuers.

Buff called the sheriff in charge of the operation. "We need hundreds of ATVs and thousands more volunteers," Buff said.

"I guess I was a step ahead of you. I put out announcements on TV and radio stations for rope, pry bars, ATVs and anything else they think we might need."

"That's great, I hope a lot of people respond," Buff said.

Twenty miles from the epicenter was the staging area for all the volunteers where they got checked in and got their equipment distributed to them. Then they were sent to all the different places where they were most needed.

Lucky found dozens of cadavers. Men went to work removing bodies, only to stop when Lucky alerted to a living person. In what had once been a huge brick home, Buff sent Lucky in and the dog alerted like someone was alive.

"Is anyone in there?" Buff cried with a sigh. He was nearly exhausted.

Someone yelled back, "Yes! We are a church group that had been meeting in the basement here. "

The back hoe showed up and cleared the first floor. After the back hoe was finished with that, Buff said, "I want you to put a four by four foot hole in the floor on the far east side. Somebody find a long, sturdy ladder and bring it to the site." To those who were trapped he yelled for them to go to the west side against the wall and wait.

The backhoe operator did as ordered. Buff yelled.

It took ten more minutes to find a ladder and get it to the site. Soon after, 24 men and women climbed out. They were all so grateful they went in turns to hug each rescuer. That made Buff very happy, but he dreaded the many days ahead when they would only be finding cadavers.

Soon two highway patrolmen with Belgian Malinois arrived on site. Buff told them where he and his team had been working and sent them out to work from there.

Buff called the sheriff and asked if they could get choppers sent in to pick up the most seriously wounded. "We'll have a dozen or so choppers heading in your direction. Keep an eye out for finding clear areas where they can land."

Soon, the choppers picked up injured people and took them by the dozens to different hospitals. Buff looked around and he could see there were more than one thousand volunteers in his area. People at their best.

For the first time, Buff noticed houses and businesses on fire a couple of blocks away. He called the fire department and was told they couldn't get to them because all the roads were impassible. He was told, "You'll just have to let them burn out. Buff could see other houses catching on fire as the fires spread. The fires spread from the structures to the grasslands and forests."

The Santa Ana winds blew in from the pacific with 30 mile per hour winds but soon a low pressure area arrived and increased the winds to 60 miles an hour, gusting to 70 MPH.

Buff was told by one of the sheriff's deputies that the quake had resulted in devastation to human civilization as far as 100 miles from the epicenter. The deputy said, "An 8.1 earthquake on the San Andreas Fault would rupture enough county utilities including Los Angeles, Riverside and San Bernardino. Two other faults under LA also slipped. It will have already caused devastation in every city in Southern California."

Shaking his head, Buff said to the deputy, "Look at the fires."

"It's hard to believe, but for miles on end buildings are on fire," the deputy told him. "We also have huge forest fires burning all over the southern part of the state."

Buff added, "There are many gas lines underground. Have you heard the multiple explosions?"

"Yes, I wasn't sure what they were," the deputy answered. "All the water lines have been ruptured so they have no water and no fire trucks to put any fires out."

"I know - it's tragic!" Buff said. "In many areas, the houses are close together; so a house on fire spreads to the houses around it."

The deputy added, "Once the fire trucks run out of gas or diesel, they can't get more. Most of the local fuel stations that I've seen are on fire or have already exploded."

Buff said, "Not long ago, they started to truck in fuel for the necessary rescue vehicles including the heavy earth movers."

A highway patrolman came up to Buff and the deputy while they were talking. The highway patrolman said, "I just heard at least 150,000 were injured, but that could be on the low side." The patrolman continued, "It's going to be much worse than that. We could lose over 25,000 more homes and 1,500 more businesses. The minimum damage estimate is 300 billion dollars."

Buff explained, "The earthquake could even cripple the national economy. We're still going to have thousands of people die in fires or even die of thirst before we can rescue them. One hundred and forty of Los Angeles hospitals are already full. They've started sending patients to hospitals in other cities and soon they will be full."

The deputy said, "Did you know that the quake destroyed the aqueducts that bring in 88% of Los Angeles' water. These aqueducts had crossed the San Andreas fault. The president has declared a national disaster for most of California."

"Yes, and they have started making plans to bus or fly people out of areas that have no water," the highway patrolman added. "This has to be the worst national disaster in America's history."

Buff, Sandy and Lucky got back to work after their break was over. Lucky alerted at a leveled home. Buff found a way in and he soon saw why Lucky had alerted. There was a dog bed filled with eight puppies and the mom. The mom looked to be part German Shepherd and Belgian Malinois. Buff was with Lucky when a helicopter pilot came up to him and said, "I've got room for the puppies and the mom in the chopper." Buff was very happy.

Lucky alerted at another home that was made of wood and wasn't terribly damaged. Buff and Lucky walked through the front door. They looked around and found themselves in the kitchen. A man was trapped under the refrigerator that had fallen apparently just as he got something out of the fridge.

Buff lifted the refrigerator off and the man crawled out from under it. He was going to have lots of bruises. Buff took him to a paramedic tent and they tended to him.

The next house that Lucky alerted on was built of brick. All the walls were down. They entered the building and Buff and Lucky went to the basement. They found four scared teens and an elderly woman who was probably their grandmother. They left the building and Buff said, "Get help from some of the rescuers waiting outside."

A policeman came up to Buff and said, "I guess you are Buff with the special dog. You're getting famous."

"What can I do for you?" Buff asked.

"Two blocks south was a huge concrete block building that totally collapsed. We're sure we're going to find many dead, but some people could still be alive."

Buff, Lucky, some volunteers and law enforcement all went to the collapsed building. Sandy was working in her own area with her team.

"What idiot would build a concrete block building that had no rebar reinforcement close to a fault line?"

The policeman said, "Cheap sons of bitches."

They went into the building and noticed that the steel girders for the building had all fallen straight down.

Every which way they looked, they saw bodies. After two hours they had found 232 dead people and no survivors. They asked the volunteers if they would bury the dead after they had gotten their names from their billfolds or purses. Buff said, "The families will have to recover their dead later, but we can't just let them rot there."

They had volunteers coming from all over with shovels. There must have been five hundred of them. They had buried the bodies by sunset.

Buff and Lucky worked for eleven days. Buff called the police chief in L.A., and he told him he had to go. Lucky's paws were cut up and sore because his booties were worn out. The chief said, "I'll get you an airplane and have it take you to wherever you want to go."

"Even to Rapid City?" Buff asked.

"No problem," said the chief. "I can't thank you enough for your coming here and for the magnificent job you've done. I hope Lucky's feet are okay."

"His feet will be fine," Buff said. "By the way, can you get the governor to send troops and National Guard troops to spread out in a 2,500 square mile area where they need the most help?"

Interstates 10, 15 and 40 crossed the fault line and were impassable. They cut off southern California from Las Vegas and Phoenix and a lot of other towns.

On the plane, in flight, on the way to Rapid City, Buff was still working. He called a friend of the chief of police who had a friend who got him in touch with the governor.

"We have a collapse of civilization here," Buff said. "We need you to call the president and tell him we need the Army, National Guard, the Marines, Air Force and the Coast Guard to be called in."

Once that was completed he felt like he had done all he could to help, and he was exhausted. He made one more call to Sandy to see if she was in an area with cell service. He found out that she wasn't.

Buff rested the last couple of hours of flight and had to be awakened when they arrived at Rapid City.

When he got to his home, he found he had dozens of calls. He decided to return the call to South Africa's head ranger right away.

The ranger told him, "My name is Ranger Dakarai. I was told you're the one to call. I wonder if you and your special dog would come here for a while and help us stop the poaching of rhinos and elephants. They are heading fast toward extinction. We have triple the number of poachers than in previous years, and now they just shoot at the rangers when we try to stop them."

Buff simply said, "I hate poachers. I can get there in a couple of days. Can I bring my own weapons?"

"I will alert the authorities that you are coming and to give you free rein. You know, more than 1,000 rhinos and 35,000 elephants have been killed over the last two years. There are only 27,000 rhinos and about 40,000 elephants left in all of Africa."

After the call, Buff set out to learn more and began searching the web. He learned that some trainers say that one Malinois with its handler can cover an area sixty times larger than the area covered by a single ranger alone.

While Buff was on the web, he ordered a special lightweight bullet proof vest for Lucky that would help his dog stay cool in the hot conditions and would still be able to stop AR-15 rounds.

As promised, Buff met head ranger Dakarai at Tambo International Airport. He had his assistant ranger with him named Bandile. After introductions were made, Dakarai said, "I'm excited to meet your dog."

"Let's go get him," Buff said.

Once they had Lucky out of the cargo area of the plane, Dakanai said, "I thought he'd be larger."

"Well, he weighs 85 pounds and can run 35 MPH," Buff replied.

In Dakarai's land rover they traveled to a distant ranger station. They were met by Kungawo, another monster of a man. Enzokahle, was a tall and fit thirty year old, and Sadeki, was a stocky man with a perpetual smile on his face.

"What do you need from us, Buff?" Dakarai asked.

"I need a high powered rifle," Buff said. "And I need to get the scent of rhinos and elephants. I need your help in setting this up."

"We have baby elephants and rhinos here," Bandile said. "We are bottle feeding them until they are big enough to return to their herd or territory."

"It's already 9 in the morning so let's get started."

"Lucky can smell elephants and rhinos from miles away if the wind is right," Buff said.

"Well here's your rifle and ammunition. Let's go find some bad guys," Bandile said.

They traveled about twenty miles and set up camp. On the third day Lucky alerted them to a rhino. Out of the blue they also saw four men armed with rifles and a chainsaw approaching the rhino which has very poor eyesight. They got a little closer and Kakarai yelled, "Stop where you are! You're all under arrest!"

One man started running and Buff said, "Take down!" Then pointed Lucky to the running poacher. In only twelve strides, Lucky was on the guy. He grabbed the guy's rifle arm and took him to the ground.

The other men surrendered. Buff yelled, "Release and Guard," and Lucky did as he was commanded. The rangers escorted the poachers back to the ranger station. There was a small jail there.

Bandile said, "Let's see if there is an elephant herd at the Creighton Water Hole."

On arrival at the water hole, Lucky was already alerting them to the elephants. Buff and Lucky found a place to hide about a hundred yards from the water hole. It was not long until ten poachers approached the herd. One of the elephants trumpeted. One of the poachers raised his rifle to kill the biggest bull.

Buff pulled out his 44 magnum and shot just over their heads. The poachers saw they were outnumbered by the rangers, but they still started shooting at them.

Buff, Chief Dakarai, Bandile and the other rangers shot back. They were all excellent shots and practiced shooting all the time. Soon there were ten dead poachers. One ranger got a flesh wound on his arm which the other rangers treated themselves.

Chief Dakarai said, "Let's go back on patrol."

On the way back as they came over a rise, they saw five men with rifles standing around a dead lion.

"Put your rifles on the ground and put your hands on the top of your head," Dakarai yelled.

The group complied. Buff and the rangers surrounded them. Kungawo yelled, "You dirty rotten sons of bitches! You better have a hunting license!"

One of the men gave Dakarai the license and he gave it to Buff. "I know we need the money from your hunts to have more money to save the rest of the lions, but you killed a lioness. I hope you feel great about killing an animal that faces extinction."

Buff, Lucky and the rangers sadly made their way back to the ranger station. Chief Dakarai had a small house and the other rangers had small huts. They built a large bonfire and sat in a circle around it.

"How many lions are left?" Buff asked.

"The government says there are only 20,000 lions left in Africa. I don't believe that. We might have 10,000. A hundred years ago there were more than 200,000 lions. The remaining lions could easily be extinct by 2050."

Dakarai rose and walked around the bonfire in front of the others. "Let's plan tomorrow's excursion. Buff, I want you to know that at least 384 African rangers have been killed since 2012. Tomorrow let's go check on the lion pride by Tamari. It is the largest pride we've seen. There are about 40 lions there at last count."

The next day they went to Tamari and Lucky alerted them two miles out. They found what was left of the pride. Half of the expected lion pride was gone.

"They sell the lions in Asia who use parts of them for medicine. The endangered lion parts they sell are bones, eyes, whiskers and teeth and are used to treat ailments. They also make wine from them and make jewelry," Dakarai said.

They continued on their excursion until they came upon a large skinned cat lying in the dirt. Chief Dakarai said, "That's a leopard."

Poachers can make 100 to 300 thousand dollars for a good leopard skin. We are also ordered to fine people who poach greater animals. I feel sorry for many of these people because they had no money for buying food in the markets. But we still have to give them a small fine.

"How much is ivory worth?" asked Buff.

"Two elephant tusks can weigh more than 250 pounds. A pound of ivory fetches as much as $1,500 on the black market. Two tusks would bring in $375,000 dollars. I'm very pessimistic that we can stop the extinction of elephants. I think people who own ivory should spend 10 years in prison. That would fix the problem," Assistant Chief Bandile said.

"The elephant ivory markets that remain open are all illegal. We need more rangers most notably in Laos, Myanmar, Thailand and Vietnam. Over 90% of the customers are estimated to hail from China. We will keep on trying to protect the endangered species, but we could use help from all over the world. We need to make people ashamed to own ivory."

The group headed for the ranger station and Lucky alerted them when they'd just started out. Lucky took them to a dead elephant with its tusks cut off. Buff said, "Let's get some of these jackasses tomorrow." Everyone agreed.

They had a big bonfire again that night. Chief Dakarai said, "If no aggressive steps are taken to save wildlife, it will not be long before they will find a place only on the list of extinct species. It will have a detrimental effect on the entire human race."

Bandile said, "259 rhinos were poached for their horns between June 27th, 2015 and June 27th, 2016. Eighty-two rhinos were poached in Kruger National Park alone. At least 25,000 elephants were killed in Africa in 2012 alone. 31 elephants were poached in Kruger in 2017. Today, on average 55 elephants are illegally killed every day."

Kungawo said, "The overall elephant population plummeted by over 20% in the past decade, mainly due to poaching for ivory. The western black rhinos were driven to extinction no matter how hard we tried to save them." In 2018, so far, Africa has experienced its worst year on record regarding ranger deaths. The game rangers association of Africa or the G.R.A.A., has reached a hundred ranger deaths on the continent since June, 2013. That means at least 1,190 African Rangers have been killed in action since 2011. We have been given orders to shoot on sight poachers in the park. We have been giving everyone notice that poachers of elephants and rhinos can be shot on sight. Buff, I don't know how you feel about that, but we have our job to do."

"If anyone shoots at me, I'll shoot back," Buff stated.

The next day they went to check a waterhole that was a favorite of the elephants. As they got close, Lucky alerted.

Six poachers approaching the herd could be seen clearly. The instant the first ranger saw a poacher raise his rifle, he fired. Soon, all six poachers were dead. Buff believed that the shoot to kill law would greatly reduce poaching.

Later that day, Buff said, "I'm heading back to the states. You're not going to have much poaching going on in Kruger National Park with those shoot on sight rules. I've got some civic duties to perform back home."

They said their goodbyes and Buff got many thanks. He headed for the airport in his borrowed Rover.

Sandy met Buff at the airport and welcomed him home from Africa in style. They stopped for an early steak dinner and went home.

They had slow, incredible sex first thing. Lucky laid outside the door, and rolled his eyes.

Later, they were in the living room snacking and watching a movie, when Buff said, "I want to take Lucky to visit nursing homes, schools, and hospices for the next two months. Lucky really needs a break."

"You're a wonderful man, Buff," Sandy said.

The next morning, Buff called the institutions and set up times that he and Lucky could visit. Almost everyone he talked to had heard of him and Lucky. Everyone he talked to said they couldn't wait for them to arrive.

They first went to a Good Samaritan Hospice. He was escorted into a room and the nurse made the introductions. They were left alone. The resident was an elderly woman named Helen and not much more than a skeleton.

"I see you brought your nice. I love dogs," the having tears in her eyes. have a muzzle on him?"dog to visit me. How woman said, already "But, how come you

"This and a couple of other places insist on it when we visit. It's good training for him to wear it once in a while. He's never shown any aggression, except that which he is trained for. He is a Law Enforcement, and Search and Rescue trained Belgian Malinois."

"He's never come close to biting anyone, that I haven't sent him after."

"I can't really pet him from here, can you take off his muzzle and have him get on the bed with me?"

"I guess there are worse ways to get fired," Buff thought. "Do you have any physical pain?"

"Of course I do, I'm old!" said the woman. "But it's nothing that could prevent me from snuggling with your puppy!"

Buff let down the railing, took off Lucky's muzzle, patted the bed, and said "Jump," and Lucky jumped on the bed.

"Lay down," Buff said and Lucky snuggled next to her. She scratched his ears and back and he rolled over for a belly rub

"Oh what a sweet dog you have!" She had a huge smile on her face.

"I'm so glad you were able to meet Lucky too!" Buff said

"I missed dogs being around me so much. Now I can die peacefully. Thank you so much for bringing him," Helen said.

"You're welcome," Buff said. "Goodbye! And I hope you live in heaven forever." Buff gave Helen a kiss on the cheek.

"You'd better go." Helen said sweetly, "I think I'm falling in love with you."

They both laughed heartily and Buff had Lucky jump down. He put her railing up and put Lucky's muzzle back on him. He and Lucky went out to the hallway. They visited many more residents.

In the next few days, Buff and Lucky went to a freshman class at Rapid City High School. The teacher introduced them to her class.

"This is Lucky and his partner, Buff." Some of the class chuckled.

"Good to see you all. I hope you're glad to see Lucky." Buff said, "Back flip," and the dog did so. There were a lot of oohs and aahs from the class.

"Hug," Buff told Lucky, and Lucky jumped up into Buff's arms. Buff hugged the dog to his chest and the students applauded.

"Is your dog dangerous?" a timid-looking student asked.

"Not as dangerous as my neighbor's Shih Tzu."

The class laughed.

"Here, look at his canines. I had titanium caps put on the canine teeth to protect his teeth so he could penetrate heavy clothing."

Buff rolled back Lucky's cheeks and he heard some say, "Cool."

"Buff is trained to attack and bite only on command. A lot of bad people are alive because he took them down before an officer had to shoot them. Often the bad guys give up right away when they see the dog."

"Who would like to come up and give some lovin' to Lucky?" Buff asked. All the student's hands went up, including the teachers.

"Please get in line and take your time. I, as your teacher, get to go first!" she said, the teacher scratched behind his ears, scratched his back, and rubbed his belly when he rolled over. Lucky loved the attention and it looked like he had a big smile on his face too.

After everyone had a turn to pet Lucky, Buff asked, "Any questions?"

"How fast can he run?" a student asked.

"Well if you're driving the 35 MPH speed limit on Mount Rushmore road, he'd be right beside you."

"How hard can he bite?"

"Lucky's bite force is 1,400 pounds per square inch. In other words, if someone put a one thousand, four hundred pound weight on one square inch of your foot, how do you think you'd feel? Everyone I've had Lucky take down has surrendered immediately. I just say, 'release and guard,' and Lucky will let go of a man's arm and lay right next to the man until I say 'come'."

When all the questions had been answered, Buff said his goodbyes and they got a round of applause and a thank you from the students. Buff headed for Saint Martin's Nursing Home.

He and Lucky arrived at 1:30 P.M. and opened the door. He saw every chair was occupied in the large living/dining area with a bunch of people having to stand.

An elderly man in a wheelchair called to Buff right away, "My God! Why are you so big!"

"I was born with Myostatin-Related Muscular hypertrophy. It made me very strong and tall. When I work out, I can get even bigger."

"I've never seen such a huge, powerful man in person," the man said.

"Thank you, this is my boss, Lucky and I'm Buff," Buff said, and then said to Lucky, "Back flip!"

Lucky happily obliged. "Hug," and Lucky jumped up into Buff's arms and he hugged him tightly to his chest. Buff put his hands under his dog's armpits and lifted him higher.

During the talk, the crowd applauded a little, and then it became a roar. They all took turns petting Lucky.

Buff decided to take Lucky on a long walk below Terry Peak, a local highly rated Ski Resort. Buff wore snowshoes and Lucky had his warm booties. Buff walked on top of the snow. Lucky was pushing through the snow up to his chest.

Buff walked on top of the berm that protected the highway. As he got to the bottom of the biggest and steepest runs, Buff heard a cracking sound. He saw an avalanche racing down the hill.

He saw that six people were right underneath where it was going to hit. They ignored the rope and sign that said, "Don't cross, Avalanche Zone."

People often crossed the Avalanche zone to get to the bottom of the next run so they could ski the other big run. Buff started trying to run in his snowshoes to the area where he just saw the people disappear.

Buff got to the bottom of the avalanche zone and told Lucky to search. Lucky alerted him right away. Buff dug through about two feet of snow and found a hand. Buff took the hand in his and pulled as hard as he could. He pulled out a girl who was coughing out snow, but she was fine.

Volunteers arrived from the main lodge and surrounding area. "Search!" Buff repeated and right away his dog alerted him to another person's location. Buff pointed and several volunteers started digging in that area.

"Search!" Lucky alerted and they dug out a man and a woman. The next time Lucky alerted and showed them where to look., one of the volunteers said, "Let's quit - nobody survives five minutes without air."

"Dig! People can stay alive in an air pocket under the snow for much longer. Don't give up!"

Sure enough, while they were digging a volunteer saw a hand sticking out of the snow. They quickly pulled out a man, but found that he had died. It was a miracle that five people were rescued unharmed. Buff and Lucky's being so close saved them for sure.

Five days later at five in the morning, Buff received a call from Bangkok. The caller said, "I'm the police chief and we need help. One-third of Thailand is flooded and we need help recovering the bodies."

"I'll grab a jet and be on the way with Lucky, my search dog."

"We have a flight booked for you and your dog in 1st class at 10 in the morning. The airline was very cooperative. Go to gate five at American Airlines and we'll see you soon." Lucky really liked all the attention he got in first class. His tail wouldn't stop wagging. He got treats and his own big water bowl, all the flight attendants and other passengers wanted to pet him.

They had to land at Ubon AFB and be taken by helicopter from there. It took a while searching to find a landing spot in Bangkok.

The Emergency Disaster Director, Randy, met Buff and asked what Lucky could do.

"Lucky can smell bodies in deep snow, water, and even mud."

The monsoon was over and soon the streets of Bangkok were draining into the ocean. On their way from the helicopter, they saw people who were walking or swimming down the street in chest-deep water. The deepest water in the Bangkok flood at the time was ten feet deep. The flood was seventeen feet deep at its highest.

Buff asked Randy what he could do first. Randy said, "Let's get in a boat and search some of the areas with the worst damage in Bangkok. Then I want us to go to a lake where two rivers meet in a small lake. There are going to be scores of dead bodies to recover there."

"Please get twenty-five real good swimmers," Buff said. "They are going to have to dive in the water with no visibility and they will have to use only their hands to find the bodies."

Ten boats had joined Buff and the director. They went house to house in one area and found many people trapped on the second floors. Boats took them to dry land. They made their way to downtown Bangkok.

Boats picked up people who were swimming in the streets. The boats took survivors to the staging areas and went back for more. Even more boats showed up. They hauled in hundreds of people stranded on rooftops, or standing in knee- deep water on the second floor of buildings.

Some were swimming in chest deep water.

Three days later, Randy, the emergency director met with Buff on one of his trips to a staging area. He said, "You're going to have one tired dog tonight."

"If we can get Lucky tired, it would be a miracle. These dogs can work all day and night and not get tired. The Malinois has the most endurance of any dog in the world. Should we go to the lake next to look for people?" Buff asked.

Once they arrived at the lake they greeted dozens of divers already waiting for them. They must have had twenty boats there. Buff pointed to a boat and said, "Can we use that boat where Lucky can stand at the front and sniff? He will need room to lie down when he alerts us to someone."

"Sure," said the Randy.

They started at the perimeter of the lake and circled around it, as they searched. Lucky would alert and they'd stop the boat every few yards it seemed like. Every few yards a diver jumped in and soon pulled a body up. Buff asked the others with boats if they could start putting the bodies in their boats. They all said, "Yes."

"Let's have two divers go down on each search," Buff suggested. They traveled another fifty feet and Lucky alerted again. They stopped the boat and two divers went into the water. They soon came up with a body and took it to a cadaver boat.

By sundown, they had pulled out seventy-six bodies. They had to call it a day. The next morning they went back to the lake and found forty-nine more bodies with Lucky's help.

Randy had set Buff up a small bungalow. He asked, "What do you think we should do, Buff?"

"I think in the morning we should start again in downtown Bangkok."

The next day it was mostly more of the same sad work. The water receded enough that they were searching in mud by the afternoon. Lucky alerted over and over, not affected by the mud at all. He jumped in and lay down many times. The dog and everyone and everything were covered in mud.

In the final counts over 2.9 million people were adversely affected. They found 815 bodies. The damage was the worst Thailand had ever experienced. Buff told the chief that he had to get home. The chief took Buff to the airport right away. Many of the divers and people from the boats showed up at the airport. They all cheered and applauded Buff and Lucky. Soon they were back on the way to Rapid City.

Buff heard a new junior high was being built at the far east side of Rapid City on city land. Buff went to a city board meeting and waited for two hours before he could speak. When his turn finally came, he stood up.

"Thank you for letting me speak. I want to put in a couple of million dollars to help build the new school, but also on the same land, I'd like to build a big, public playground. In turn, I'd like you to let me build a dog training center in the same area. It would have ten-foot high chain link fencing enclosing about eight acres.

"First, I'd buy $32,000 dollars' worth of training equipment for training for at least eight events. It includes a big slide, a chain net, a net climber, a double side transfer station, a straight slide, a spiral slide, and plenty of room to move around in tunnels. The training center would be used for me to bring up a trainer for a week or two to teach the highway patrol dogs how to search, how to search on water, to attack with a hand signal, and how to sniff out alive or dead bodies.

"We'll have an eight-foot wall, a six-foot wall, and a four-foot wall. We'll have a ladder they need to climb and then go down the slide.

"We'll have two hemp ropes tied to platforms off the ground about one and a half feet apart. Here we will train them to walk thirty feet from one platform to another.

"At the new playground, there will be climbers, seesaws, double walled slides and swing sets, a spinner pendulum swing, ramps and platforms. Sit and spin teeter totters and a merry go round. I'll add other things as needed. Thank you for your time."

The director of the city council said, "I love the idea and hope we can work it out. We'll have an answer at the next meeting two weeks from today."

"I'll look forward to the next meeting then," Buff said.

At the next council meeting they took up Buff's request. "They voted YES unanimously. We want to thank you for sharing your money with us to get it done. The kids will go wild when they see the playground."

Later, Buff got on the phone and started ordering what he needed. He called all over the country if needed to get the playground equipment on the way. He hired Rand Construction to build the playground and the dog training center.

He called the head of the highway patrol and told him about the training center. Carl, the chief said, "Hell yes! We want in. Our dogs should receive extra training and not just sniff out drugs and run down fugitives."

Soon after the center was completed, many dogs, mostly Belgian Malinois and a few German Shepherds, came from many other states to get extra training.

It was such a success that Buff hired a full time dog trainer that specialized in the Malinois breed. Hiring a man would cost him $90,000 a year. Soon, other states started building training centers and Buff was so happy that the dogs were being trained for what they seemed to be born to do.

The trainer, Judd Henry told Buff that the German Shepherd was usually very friendly with other dogs, but they aren't as fast or as agile as Malinois.

One day, the trainer, Judd pulled Buff aside and said, "Thank you for the dream job."

"You're welcome, and I couldn't be happier with having you here."

On their way back to Rapid City, Sheriff Carlyle called. Since Sandy was driving, Buff answered.

"We have a sniper on top of the Orin-Jensen Hotel. He has shot eight people so far. We can't get close enough to rescue anyone so I don't even know if anyone survived. I talked to the Rapid City Police Chief and we agreed that you should be in charge."

"So now, I'm your unpaid Chief Deputy Sheriff again?" Buff asked.

"God, I hope so," Sheriff Carlyle said with a smile in his voice. "Thanks for all your free help, Buff."

"I just happen to be close to the scene right now," Buff said. "I'll be there in minutes."

Sandy heard the conversation over the car's speaker and headed that way before the conversation ended. They parked about a block away, where one of the roadblocks had been set up.

Buff, Sandy and Lucky got dressed in their bullet proof vests and jogged down the street. Lucky obediently followed Buff closely. They could hear a lot of gunfire. They met the chief of police at the corner of the Eastwood Restaurant. They could peek around the corner from there and could see most of the bodies lying on the sidewalks and one in the middle of the street.

The S.W.A.T. team showed up minutes after Buff did. As they got out of the S.W.A.T. van, Buff asked, "How many of you are snipers?" Two men raised their hands.

"I'm Deputy Sheriff Means and I'm in charge here. Would you two find a way to get on the roofs of the two buildings across the street from the hotel? One of you take the six story building and the other go to the seven story building."

A police officer came up to Buff and said, "I heard you were in charge. The man on the roof is William Durst. He just got out of prison where he spent ten years on attempted murder charges."

"Oh crap!" Buff exclaimed. "I know William well. He's a bad man."

Buff got a bullhorn from the S.W.A.T. team and asked them to start up the fire escape to the roof of the hotel. "Wait to hear from me once you get there. The snipers are probably in place now. They will radio us. I'm pretty sure in William's case, they will have to take him out."

He put the bullhorn in front of his face and yelled, "Durst! You are surrounded and you did your damage. Put your rifle down and go to the door."

Durst fired ten shots at the street. He hit a highway patrolman who had been hiding behind his motorcycle on the street. All of the law enforcement officers fired back, but Durst only had to duck down behind a three foot wall that went all the way around the top of the hotel.

"Come on down, Durst," Buff yelled again. "Give up - you don't want to die."

"I'm not going back to prison!" Durst screamed.

Buff contacted the snipers and said, "Take him out as soon as you get a chance."

Around ten minutes later, Durst popped up and started shooting down at the street again. Both snipers fired and hit him squarely in the forehead. Durst just stood there for a second, and then he and his gun took a nosedive off the hotel. The sound of him hitting the ground was sickening. Durst landed on his head and crumpled in half. The sounds of bones shattering could be heard by anyone near.

Buff walked up to Durst's body as a bellboy peeked out of the hotel's front door. "Get me two sheets and help me cover him." Buff said to the bellboy. The young man took off to get the sheets. Buff looked across the street and noticed that three news teams were filming. The bellboy came right back out with the sheets.

Buff covered the body. The bellboy threw up after seeing what was left of Durst. Red streaks soaked the sheets right away.

Ambulances started pouring into the street for the EMTs and paramedics to check the victims. The patrolman who had been shot, and three others were the only survivors. They were rushed to the hospital with lights and siren.

A newscaster from KRUN suddenly yelled at Buff, "Did you have to kill the guy?"

"Hell yes! We had to kill him, and that's all I have to say now except I'm telling you all to leave now, or I'll arrest you for obstructing!" Buff yelled back.

The news people were escorted to their vans and invited to leave again by other law enforcement personnel. The medical examiner took Durst's body to the morgue. There was no doubt about his cause of death, but they still had to do an autopsy.

Buff was tired of Rapid City getting so much bad publicity. But he knew in his heart that Rapid City was probably still one of the safest cities in the country.

Buff and Sandy were driving into Keystone at six in the morning to inspect how much damage the big flood had done the night before. The flood waters were so strong they tore out the 1880s train tracks for miles

Buff got a call on the radio. It was the sheriff. He said, "You've got an upside-down truck with only the undercarriage showing above the flood waters a few miles up Hill City Road."

"10-4," Buff said and hung up the mic. Sandy gave him a concerned look. They hurried to the site. The Keystone Volunteer Firefighters were already there. An old friend of Buff's, Lisa, was on the scene and ran up to him when he and Sandy pulled up. Buff got out of the truck while Sandy waited inside with Lucky.

"That's Jeff's truck! He was coming down Old Hill City Road on his way home. His truck hit that muddy strip of sludge covering the road and just slipped into the creek. The force of the water pushed it over and it ended up like it is."

Buff knew Jeff and his father and had done some work with them in the past. The upside down truck was about eight feet from the river bank. Buff leapt to the truck and grabbed onto the undercarriage. His feet were swept out from under him and he was left just hanging on by one hand.

He pulled himself back to the truck and got a good fist hold on the undercarriage. Buff tried to kick out the driver's side window, but the running water made it impossible even for Buff.

Jake, a big guy with the Keystone Fire Department, jumped in next to Buff. He yelled at the firemen on the bank, "Get us a long pry bar and a small sledgehammer."

The chief of the fire department jumped out to the upside down truck with the requested equipment. He gave the pry bar to Buff and he gave Jake the sledgehammer.

Buff placed the end of the pry bar in the gap by the door's locking mechanism and Jake pounded it in. Buff pulled on the pry bar and the metal door just bent. The truck even moved a bit with Buff's strength.

Jake yelled at Buff, "Get it right on the door latch!"

Buff yelled back, "What do you think I'm trying to do?" He put the pry bar farther down, but he couldn't see where the door latch was because of the swirling muddy water.

Jake pounded on the bar again and reached over Buff's back to pull on the bar with him. The door opened two inches; Buff grabbed the door and pulled against the swirling water. He got it open some more, and Jake kept it from closing again. Buff dived down into the flooded truck and found an arm. He pulled the man he found close enough to shore so the others could get him into the ambulance and start CPR.

Lisa watched closely, and suddenly yelled, "That's not Jeff!"

Buff yelled back, "I know!"

Buff looked over to the road and saw one of the volunteer firemen drive up with his logging machine. Buff and Jake crawled up on the bank and the logging machine driver opened the giant mouth of the machine and rolled the truck upright.

Buff and Jake moved in quickly and pulled their friend Jeff out. They got him to the riverside and handed him off to the ambulance crews. Buff and Jake sat down in the mud on the bank, breathing hard.

The paramedics started CPR and soon shocked Jeff. They slammed the ambulance doors and rushed him with lights and siren to the Regional Health Emergency Room. The doctors and nurses worked on Jeff for forty minutes in total. Buff knew he was gone even before he left the scene.

The hospital staff put all of the ambulance crew, the firemen, and Search and Rescue in a large room for critical incident debriefing. Reverend Cleveland asked each person to speak about Jeff.

One woman said, "He was the nicest guy anybody could have known."

Another woman said, "He was a great EMT - I worked closely with him for years."

Most of the people at the debriefing spoke. Buff just said a sentence or two, similar to what had already been said. They were still in shock when the debriefing ended. The staff and rescuers went into the ER and took a look at Jeff. His skin was white except for the large bruise on his forehead. Buff said softly, "It looks like Jeff had been knocked out, so at least he didn't suffer."

They had a huge funeral with a few hundred people attending. After the funeral, Buff walked over to Jeff's father and offered his condolences. His father said, "I know you loved my son, and you did everything humanly possible to save him."

Sandy was driving on a Saturday night. Buff and Sandy routinely patrolled the area when they weren't on a rescue or searching for bodies on a reservation.

Dispatch called and asked Buff and Sandy if they were close to Lovies. Buff picked up the mic and reported their location. "We're just a few blocks away."

"We have a report that there is a big fight going on - please respond," the dispatcher said.

Sandy checked her mirrors and sped up. Buff acknowledged the call and turned around in his seat. He put the bulletproof vest on Lucky, and he got his own vest on. Sandy was already wearing her vest and was armed.

Sandy stopped hard enough to skid the tires in front of the entrance and they jumped out. Buff positioned himself on one side of the door, Sandy, and Lucky on the other. The two pulled their weapons.

Buff nodded and the three burst through the door. Lucky stopped in front of them and sat down looking back at Buff. There was no fight going on. The place was dark except for the glowing neon light behind the bar.

The only person that they saw at first was the guy they beat up at the 7th avenue bar years ago, and soon seven new henchmen stepped out from behind the bar to back him up. They were all rather large bikers dressed to the max.

"So glad you could make it, Sheriff. I missed you," the man said.

"Hey, long time no see," Buff said. "I see you have seven new guys with you. I wonder what happened to your other friends," Buff said using a sing-song voice.

"I've brought with me seven martial artists with black belts. Now you're in deep shit!" the biker leader said. "I'll take care of that little blonde wife of yours myself."

"Well big guy," Sandy stepped forward and angrily said, "You can try - you bastard!"

"My gang is gonna beat Means so badly he'll wish he was never born - and when I'm done with you, you'll want to die."

"Bring it on," Buff said.

The big biker rushed Sandy. She ran farther inside and away from the door. The boss biker chased her and she met him with a flying side-kick that connected with the side of his head.

He went down moaning. A trickle of blood showed near his temple. Sandy taunted him. "Are you sure you don't want to give up?"

"Give up - hell. I'm still going to kick your ass." He threw a punch at Sandy's nose. She easily stepped aside and he missed. She smoothly turned and elbowed him in his nose. Blood came gushing out. He got up only angrier.

She did a jumping roundhouse kick which connected again in the side of his head. He almost went down. "Boy, you sure have a hard head!" Sandy said. He got up again and she planted her knee right in his balls. He went down screaming

The other seven bikers rushed at Buff, he braced himself, and Lucky knew what was coming. He leaped forward and sunk his enhanced teeth into the lead opponent. The guy went to his knees.

The next guy received a punch to his gut and he went down. The next guy got Buff's fist against the side of his head. The fourth guy found Buff's foot colliding with his head after Buff did a spinning roundhouse kick.

There were still three guys left, and they hesitated. Lucky was back at Buff's side. Buff head butted the fifth guy and at the same time scooped up the sixth guy in his left arm. As he came up from the head butt, he threw the sixth guy over the counter. The seventh guy was cornered by Lucky. Buff looked around to see where Sandy was.

He took a sharp breath when he saw her. The boss biker had his arm around her chest, a knife to her throat.

"Stop now, Sheriff. I think I've won here."

Of the other seven bikers, those that could still stand, got up and rather feebly held onto Buff's arms.

"Let her go you fucking moron of a jackass," Buff screamed.

"No way. You will die. But first, you'll watch her die."

Buff froze in shock. Sandy's worried eyes glanced at Buff, as the Boss Biker pressed his knife hard, sinking it deeply into her neck. Then looking at Buff, he pulled the knife across her throat. There was a hint of a smile on Sandy's lips for Buff, just before her head rolled back, blood coming out of her neck like a red waterfall, instantly soaking her uniform shirt

Buff roared. He easily threw off the guys who thought they were holding his arms.

Buff kicked the closest guy in the knee. His knee buckled backward, and he screamed and went to the floor, not to get up again. He wasn't going to be fighting anyone for a long time.

A biker punched Buff in the side from behind. Buff just stood up straight and turned to face the man. A large wet stain formed on the front of the man's pants. Buff just gave him an eye strike to put him down. He didn't really want to touch the man with the wet pants at all. He would have laughed at him, but he was enraged over what happened to Sandy.

He pushed another guy hard enough to send him flying over the counter and when his head hit the wall, it went all the way through. His head and shoulders were outside the building.

Two guys came at him and Buff jumped high and kicked both in the face at the same time.

The next one got a punch in the gut that fractured his liver. He went down, already pale from internal bleeding.

Buff turned to look for the boss. He was standing over Sandy's bloody body. Buff started toward the Boss.

The last guy standing behind him tried to grab him. Buff grabbed his arm and flipped him over his shoulder. Once on the ground, he punched him in the chest hard enough to stop the guy's heart.

Watching Buff and seeing the expression on his face as he walked toward him, the boss cried, Pplease, I give up! I'll do whatever you want!"

"I only want you to die for what you did to my WIFE!!!" Buff screamed.

The boss screamed as he turned to run. Buff barely missed grabbing the boss's foot when he hesitated to step over Sandy's body.

He followed the running man back out to the parking lot. Six patrol cars with lights flashing pulled in and all skidded to a stop when they saw the Boss running from Buff across the parking lot.

Sheriff Carlyle jumped from his car in front of the runner. The boss ran right into the sheriff's arms. The other deputies now surrounded Buff, the boss, and the sheriff. Buff was still after the boss. Buff still wanted to kill the man.

He carefully got in front of Buff and held out his hand to stop him. Buff only roared and made fists with his hands. Buff didn't even recognize Sheriff Carlyle.

"Buff STOP!! We got him!" Sheriff Carlyle said forcefully.

Buff growled and pushed Carlyle to the side with one hand. The deputies holding the boss moved their prisoner around behind the last patrol car in the row. Buff kept coming, so they put the boss in the back seat of the car and locked the doors.

Sheriff Carlyle followed Buff, trying again to get in front of him to stop him, but Buff just ignored him.

Buff went around to the same side of the car where they put their prisoner. The deputies tried to stop him, and he swatted them away like flies.

In the car, the boss screamed, got as far from that side of the car as he could, and squeezed his eyes shut.

Buff found the door locked, so he put his fist through the patrol car's rear passenger-side window. Blood gushed from his wrist, and he felt pain. Those watching could see him calming down. Buff relaxed his fists. From behind him, Sheriff Carlyle put his hand carefully and gently on Buff's shoulder. Carlyle felt Buff relax some more.

Suddenly Buff screamed, "He killed her! He killed Sandy. My WIFE. He should die!" Buff went to his knees.

"Oh God, Buff. I'm so sorry! Now I understand why you acted the way you did." Carlyle tried to comfort Buff. To the deputies, he said, "Go inside and start the investigation."

Carlyle continued, "Buff please, come to my car and have a seat. Just take a few deep breaths." Buff walked calmly. He did as he was told. He couldn't do anything else right then.

Once sitting in the car, Buff started sobbing. Carlyle kneeled next to him and put his hand on Buff's knee. He said, "When you're ready, tell me what happened. And if you need anything let me know. I'll do it if I can. "

Sheriff Carlyle watched over the investigation. He had a deputy stay with Buff while he went inside for a short time. The medical examiner showed up and Sheriff Carlyle spoke to him privately outside for a few minutes before they went back inside. Ambulances showed up and they started to bring out the bodies.

Buff noticed the bodies were being moved and he got out of the car. He pushed past the deputy to find Sandy's body. It was easy to see which body was the smallest in the body bags. He unzipped the bag and looked into her face. Buff gently closed her eyelids and started sobbing again.

It took a while, but Sheriff Carlyle got Buff away from the gurney and they loaded her in the vehicle.

Sheriff Carlyle got Buff back in his patrol car and took him to the station. There was no way he would let him go home alone even if they had to tranquilize him.

"Do you have anyone you can call, Buff?"

"Yes, I have a good friend next door that will come over," Buff said. A deputy took Buff home and made sure his neighbor was there before he left.

Since he lost Sandy, Buff hadn't been working out as hard as he had been. He had only practiced martial arts every day since. That helped him feel better. He was starting to feel worse and worse missing Sandy. After she died, at some point, he knew he wasn't taking good care of himself. He even noticed he tired more easily than he used to.

He decided to go for three world records in power lifting. He might have been just trying to distract himself from his pain, but no matter what, he felt better when he was working out hard.

Buff weighed 349 pounds. He called the sheriff and told him he would be off work for a year to compete in the world weightlifting championship. The sheriff understood and was glad he was taking some time off.

"Just give me a call when you want to come back to work for us," Sheriff Carlyle said.

"Sure," Buff said sadly.

Over the next few months, Buff worked out for as many as 7 hours a day. His bench press was up to 750 pounds. He only had to lift 33 pounds more to break the world record. His squat was 990 pounds, and he only had to lift 90 pounds more. His deadlift was 1,100 pounds which was only five pounds less than the record.

In two more month she was ready for the Minneapolis Worldwide Weightlifting competition. After he arrived, he was astounded at how huge the other lifters were. There were only three men trying for the record in the bench press. Four men were trying for the deadlift and three men for the squat.

The contest started, and Buff walked up to the bench press first. He approached a bar that weighed 790 pounds. He made the lift and would soon have the world record if nobody else could lift it. The other men tried to lift 800 pounds and failed to complete the lift.

Three men tried to lift 1,115 pounds in the deadlift. The first three failed. Buff approached the bar after chalking his hands and lifted the weight without hesitation. The crowd cheered. Buff was now the world champion in the deadlift and the bench press.

Now all that was left was the squat. He lifted 1,080 at home. It would have been a world record if witnessed. Buff waited for the two men to try to lift 1,100 pounds and both failed. Buff felt a little bubbly inside. He was either nervous or ecstatic or both. He chalked up and approached the bar. He asked to have weight added. Now the bar weighed 1,150 pounds. At first, as he tried, it didn't look like he was going to be able to do it.

The audience was silent as they held their breath. Suddenly, he made it to a standing position. He stood straight up and held it!

Now, Buff was officially the strongest man in the world. The parties went on all night. He slipped out and went to his hotel room at about 11:30 in the evening. As happy as he was at winning. He still cried himself to sleep thinking about Sandy. It just wasn't time yet for him to stop mourning.

Buff flew back to Rapid City the next morning and he was surprised by the city having a parade in his honor. Thousands lined the sidewalks downtown. Buff enjoyed it, but was filled with thoughts of Sandy and his life.

He found himself thinking about how he was through with competitive weightlifting. He decided during the parade that he would again focus on helping people with Lucky at his side. He felt very good about the decision. He decided he'd get from 349 pounds down to 325 at least to start.

Buff felt like he was ready to get back to work.

Buff was hanging out at the sheriff's office with Lucky when a call came in that a pawn shop was being robbed. An officer named Doug raced with Buff to the pawn shop

Doug was a tall skinny officer who's uniform always looked a little baggy. He had blond hair and freckles splashed across his nose. He was always sucking on a lollipop. He said it was like his mentor, Kojak, an old TV show about a detective.

Doug stopped the car, silently about 30 feet from the front door. They crept closer and had cover behind nearby dumpsters if they needed it. Buff shouted, "Sheriff's office! Come out now! You are under arrest."

The two burglars ran out of the back door with each man carrying duffle bags stuffed with the most valuable stuff they could find. "Stop where you are or I'm sending the dog!" Buff yelled.

The men dropped their bags and Buff told them to turn around and put their hands behind their backs. They both did so and Doug and Buff flex-cuffed them. Buff opened their bags and found 15 AR-15s, and dozens of pistols and ammo. The sheriff showed up in his car and went around back to find his men.

"Good job you guys," he said. "Thank you. I'm so glad you captured them. They had a lot of weapons that won't go to the streets now."

Thinking about Sandy and all of his feelings that were still going strong, months after her death, Buff called Craig Jones. He told him that he heard he knew a very spiritual man who had a school about Edgar Cayce and Ross Peterson's readings.

Edgar Cayce and Ross Peterson could be led into a trance, leave their bodies and give what they called readings to any person in any part of the world. The readings were mostly about health, but they gave readings on past lives, strengths, and weaknesses.

Craig said, "Well, Buff, I have a friend in Minneapolis who had the school. His name is Joseph Cannon. His phone number is 625 853 1517. Tell him hello for me."

Buff called Joseph and told him about his wonderful experience with the Lakota Medicine Men and other Holy Men. "I would like to know more about God," Buff said.

"Well, let's set up an appointment and I'll see you soon," Joseph said. They set a meeting for two weeks from that day. Lucky stayed home and Buff went alone.

Buff flew his Beechcraft into the Minneapolis airport, grabbed a cab and he was soon in front of Joseph's house.

As he stood before the house, Buff thought it was what you could call almost a mansion. The big oak double doors had a knocker on them so Buff used it.

A nice-looking 60-year-old man answered the door. He said, "You must be Buff Means. I've heard of some of your and Lucky's adventures. I'm Joseph Cannon and we have a three-hour talk scheduled."

"How did you get interested in Cayce?" Buff asked.

"Thirty-five years ago, a friend of mine told me to read the book, *There is a River*," Joseph said.

"That's the first book about him that I read too," Buff said. "I was hooked. I've never heard anyone or read anything that explains the nature of God as Cayce did. His readings read absolutely true to me. I read some of Cayce's books 25 years ago. Now I realized, I don't remember much of what he had to say. I remember thinking, how Cayce must be very close to God. I hope you can help me out because I'm really struggling with depression since my wife died," Buff admitted.

"For God's sake, come in. I was so intrigued by your story that I forgot to invite you in right away." Joseph gestured through a large open archway. "Here, follow me."

They went into a monstrous living room that was absolutely gorgeous. There was a huge stone fireplace and a chandelier, and it was the most beautiful room he'd ever seen. Everything fit like it was made to go together, just for that house.

"Joseph, how long have you taught about Cayce and Peterson's teachings?" Buff asked.

"About twenty-five years."

"Joseph, I really would like to pay you for today's session."

Joseph said, "Absolutely not. Any friend of Craig Jones is my friend too."

Buff said, "So you have private groups four days a week and you set aside time for a day of individual sessions?"

"You've got it absolutely right. It keeps me busy and I think I can help people."

There was a knock on the front door and Joseph said, "That must be Nancy. She works with me as well. I will conduct her into a trance."

Nancy, a short, dark-haired middle-aged woman came into where the men were talking. Joseph made introductions.

"Nancy, this is Buff, Buff, Nancy." They had a good handshake and Nancy went to the couch where she was going to do a reading. She laid down, closed her eyes, and appeared to be relaxing her whole body.

Joseph sat next to her and said, "Please clear the mind and tell us when the mind is clear."

After two minutes Nancy said, "The mind is clear."

Joseph said, "Dear Lord, please protect this entity and all forms of entities from all negative influences, regardless of source, and give up the answers we all seek of this inquiring mind through the manifestation of truth, intelligence, and love - Amen."

"Would you please allow both body and mind to go to whom to where to what and to when it is directed?" Joseph said.

"Please tell us about the form of Buff Means, located at 1920 West Blue Rd, Minneapolis Minnesota, and tell us when you have located the same."

"We have the body," Nancy said.

"Please remove all harmful influences from this entity at this time," Joseph said. He turned to Buff and said, "You can ask questions now."

"What is the purpose of my life?" Buff asked.

Nancy answered, "Your job is to rescue and save people from catastrophes and to teach people about the Oneness of life."

"What is the lump on the back of my neck?" Buff asked.

"It is a cyst and you can easily have it surgically removed," Nancy replied.

"Is Lucky the best-trained Belgian Malinois in the world?" Buff asked.

"He definitely is. He is a most beautiful and special dog. He can do some things that other dogs can't even try. He can climb a ten-foot wall where only 1 in 100 Belgian Malinois can."

"What is the pain in my lower left stomach?" Buff asked.

"Your appendix is inflamed. It will rupture in a week unless you have it removed," Nancy answered.

"Have I suffered brain damage from all the blows I've taken on my head?" Buff asked.

"Yes. Your concussions have caused a small amount of damage. It's nothing that will disable you."

"How is my health overall?" Buff asked.

"Your health is good other than what I previously mentioned."

Joseph asked if Buff was done and he said, "Yes."

Joseph instructed Nancy, "Please remove all negative and harmful influences from this force and entity at this time."

Nancy answered, "Done."

Joseph told Nancy, "Please allow any healing which may take place at this time."

Nancy said, "Done."

"Please allow all bodily functions to slowly and gently return to normal, ensuring that all gates are returned to the normal state and position, allowing the mind to recall all dreams and impressions."

"Done," Sandy said.

"Please allow both body and mind to awaken feeling completely refreshed, whole, integrated and aware," Joseph said.

"Done." Nancy woke up with a stretch and a yawn.

She asked, "Did you get what you wanted?"

"Yes," Buff said. "Even more than I wanted."

"You'd better get surgery in the next few days," Joseph reminded him.

"You'd better believe I will."

Buff and Joseph said their thanks and farewells to Nancy who was leaving.

Joseph's cell phone rang and he answered, "This is he whom you are speaking to."

"This is Jan - they need you at the VA locked ward because one of your clients who is suffering from Major Depression is acting out."

"Okay Jan, I'll be there." Joseph agreed and put his phone away. "Buff, I need to go to the VA soon. I can still give you an hour."

"I understand," Buff said. "That will be fine."

"I've got five pages of quotes here, and I'm going to read as much as I can in the hour we have left."

Buff asked what was the most important thing he should know. Joseph turned a page and read one of Cayce's readings.

"The first lesson you teach anyone for six months should be the principle of One - One, one; Oneness of God, Oneness of man's relationship to God. Oneness of Force, Oneness of Time, Oneness of Purpose, Oneness in every effort, oneness, oneness."

Joseph read that Cayce said, "The creative energy wants us to be companionable to and cocreators with him. All things that are in the universe are constantly in motion, vibrating. That includes mountains and rocks and everything else."

"All energy is electrical in its manifested form. The vibrating force is the active force. It is the active principle that all radiate from. But the observation that is created is from the life energy itself. All power, all force is what is termed God Consciousness."

"No one should put country before the Fatherhood of God and the Brotherhood of man. Upon time and space are written the thoughts, deeds, and activities of each of us. It is called the akashic record, which is God's book of a person's life."

"Don't think that your life isn't being written in the book of life? I found it! I have seen it. It is being written. You are the writer."

"There is no death passing through God's other door, energy is just passing into the spiritual plane. It is the birth and beginning of a new spiritual life. The idea we can all share is to love God with all your body, your mind, and your soul and love your neighbor as yourself."

"This is the answer to the problems as they exist in the world today."

Joseph continued reading quotes by Cayce. "Be at peace, be in harmony with the constructive, creative forces. Life in all its manifestations, in every animate force, are the creative forces in action. Vibration is created of the same energy as life itself. All power - all force is what is termed *God consciousness*."

"I've thought that for decades," Buff said. "When I heard God's voice telling me that someday you'll heal with your hands, hopefully I will or already have. I don't know if I've saved 100 or 200 people. I won't ever know for sure."

When Buff got back to Rapid City he called his doctor and told him the story. Dr. Morton said, "I've never heard of readings just like that, but I'll check out your appendix. Lay there on the treatment table."

Buff did as he was told. The doctor palpated his appendix area very hard causing Buff to groan.

"How painful was that?" Morton asked.

"It was painful enough," Buff said.

"Well, your appendix has to go. It's good you found out about it when you did, however, you found out," Dr. Morton said.

They took Buff to surgery right away, and soon he was looking at a bandage on his right lower quadrant. He felt good and was in almost no pain. He stayed in the hospital for two days and had several visitors. Even Nancy came by from Minneapolis.

When Buff arrived home, he took a couple of days easy. At least for him, he thought he was taking it easy. First, he did a training session with Lucky. Later, he was at his desk when Ed Hermanson, the Minot Sheriff, called.

"We've all heard about you and your Belgian Malinois," Ed began. "We need some help."

Sheriff Hermanson continued, "We've had 15 overdoses in the last week. We have two reservations with populations of 8,700 and 28,000 and we have two meth labs that need to be taken down. About 50 percent of the people on the rez are addicted to meth."

"They are making some of the meth look like candy so kids will quickly take them too."

"Fucking evil people!" Buff muttered so the caller couldn't hear. "I'll see you at the airport tomorrow at 10 in the morning and we will come up with a plan," Buff said.

The next morning he met with Sheriff Hermanson as promised. There were also several Deputies and several highway Policemen with their trained Belgian Malinois. They let the dogs get acquainted and then the sheriff told Buff about two meth labs out in the boondocks, but they can't get a search warrant.

Buff asked if he could talk to the judge. The sheriff said, "I'm sure we can arrange it."

The next day Buff was in the judge's quarters early. He told the Judge about what he and his dog had done. Judge Davis said, "I've heard of you and your dog, but why should I give you a search warrant?"

"I got a search warrant before when Lucky alerted me to drugs being present. Your reservation has the highest meth use per capita in the country. You have fifteen Natives dead already this year and it's going to get worse."

"So if Lucky alerts on these meth operations, you want me to give you search warrants."

"Yes," said Buff. "My dog has never been wrong."

"Okay, if Lucky alerts on both sites I'll give you warrants for both places. You better be right or I'm going to be in trouble."

The sheriff, Buff, Lucky, and a few Deputy Sheriffs went to the sites at midnight. Both labs had covered windows, so there was no danger of being seen if they did it right. They snuck up on the labs and Lucky alerted at both places.

Law enforcement had a big meeting and they made their plans. During the meeting, Buff took the lead.

"The ground is flat, so I think we need to have an overwhelming force and drive fifteen vehicles to each place. We will surround the places from about fifty meters away. Hide between your vehicles. I'll use a bullhorn and tell them to surrender, but the last two times I did that and they opened fire," Buff said.

Buff continued, "Have all the law enforcement vehicles point their bright lights on the buildings. Now we have to get thirty or more officers to sign on."

The highway patrol volunteered eight cars. The police chief from Minot rounded up more vehicles. All the officers were given AR-15s.

At the planned time, law enforcement vehicles surrounded both labs. At the big meth lab barn, Buff yelled in the bullhorn and told them they were surrounded and to come out with their hands on top of their heads. They waited a few seconds before nine men and one woman came out as instructed. They were all handcuffed and put in vehicles.

"Buff, the sheriff, and many officers went into the lab. They found a thousand pounds of meth, two hundred pounds of Fentanyl, and four hundred pounds of marijuana. They called the police department and asked them to make arrangements to transport the drugs."

Twenty miles away, they had surrounded the other big meth lab. The head of the highway patrol, Tom Collins, called on the bullhorn, "We have you surrounded, come out with your hands in the air!"

Bullets started flying out of the large lab. One guy ran for it and a highway patrolman told his dog, "Take him down."

The dog soon had the man screaming. All the officers started firing at the muzzle flashes from inside the lab. They knew that they had killed a couple of the suspects, but then a huge explosion tore the place apart and flames shot in the air a hundred feet. They had a fire truck on standby so it was there quickly. The firemen were able to keep it from spreading, but the lab was burned to the ground.

They found traces of drugs and nine human remains. They bagged the drugs and called the medical examiner and the coroner to come to the scene.

They got a couple of trucks and took the bodies to the medical examiner's van. They took the drugs that had somehow escaped the flames to the Police command tent that they had set up. The officers started to search and identify the bodies. Some had wallets that had IDs in them.

Those bodies whose fingers hadn't been burned were fingerprinted.

They soon got results and three men were felons. The medical examiner was busy taking impressions of their teeth to try to identify them from dental records. Many of them would never be identified.

The chief of police, the sheriff, and the chief of the highway patrol came to Buff to thank him. The chief of police said, "We only had one highway patrolman with a gunshot right through his leg. They patched him up and he will be fine. Thank you so much."

Buff was heading home on Highway 16 when he heard the dispatcher say, "Anyone by Highway 16 Wye - please go to the accident on Highway 16 two miles from the Keystone Wye." Buff pushed down on the gas. He drove a hundred miles an hour on his way to the wreck.

Three guys were standing around. The big guy called out, "We need a backhoe or something to get this car off of him."

Buff said, "Come on, we can lift it together!"

The big guy said, "Those cars weigh over 2,000 pounds! We can't lift that!"

"I can raise around a thousand pounds alone, and we don't have to lift the whole car. We only have to tip it up enough to pull this guy out from under it."

While Buff spoke, another car stopped and a small young man asked Buff if he could help. "Sure, when we tip the car up off of him, grab him by both hands and pull him free."

The five men lifted the side of the car about two feet up and the small guy pulled him out. The Rapid City fire department, and ambulance service, pulled up and quickly jumped out of their vehicles. The lead paramedic asked Buff what they had.

Buff told them that the driver apparently lost control and obviously he wasn't wearing a seatbelt. The paramedics checked out his back and started to hoist him onto the gurney. Buff saw them and yelled, "Stop! He may have broken his lumbar vertebrae. I don't think you should turn him over. The head paramedic went to the ambulance to call the ER. He asked for a doctor. The doctor soon came on the radio and said, "What can I do for you?" The paramedic told him what had happened and the doctor said if he was breathing okay and had a good heart rate, to bring him in on his stomach. If he crashes, you'll have to turn him over and shock him. The paramedic told everybody what had been said; so they all carefully lifted him onto the gurney on his front. Buff asked if he could follow them to the hospital and keep track of how their patient is doing. Everyone there agreed.

At the hospital, Buff waited in the ER for two hours before the surgeon came in and asked, "Who is Buff?"

"I am," Buff said, raising his hand.

The surgeon said, "The patient has five fractures of his lumbar vertebrae but he can still move his extremities; so he isn't paralyzed. It's going to be a very long recovery; so you might as well go home. Buff asked, "Could you give me a call and tell me how he's doing?" Buff handed the surgeon his card. They said their goodbyes and Buff went back to work.

After work, Buff and Lucky were lying on the couch together and Buff was watching a movie. His mobile phone rang.

"This is the party to whom you are speaking," Buff answered.

The doctor said, "Well, you better be Buff or I'm hanging up."

"No, don't hang up! I thought it was the sheriff calling."

"Well, good enough then," the doctor said. "As far as we can tell at this stage the guy you brought in will make a complete or nearly complete recovery."

Buff thanked the doctor. He was glad that the man would be okay. He saw so many injured people that it was nice to check on them sometimes.

The doctor said, "It's good you didn't turn him over. He would have been paralyzed for sure."

A few weeks later, Buff got a call from Sheriff Carlyle and he told Buff that a guy on the back of Mount Rushmore, close to the unfinished hall of records, was having a severe heart attack. Buff was already in Keystone; so he was only minutes from Mount Rushmore.

When he arrived at the entrance he saw a ranger standing next to a gate. He introduced himself. "We heard you've got a man having a heart attack behind the faces. Will you call Search and Rescue and two ambulances from Keystone?"

"Will do," the ranger said. "Go on up, and good luck." Buff climbed the back of the monument's 50-foot aluminum ladder that is attached to the granite. He climbed to the top and was soon behind the faces. There were 12 contractors there just standing around.

Buff went to the man who was on a stretcher in the shade. Buff said, "Please move him into the sunlight."

The contractors quickly moved the man. Buff felt the man's pulse and found it to be weak and thready. He told the man on the stretcher, "I'm Pennington County Deputy Sheriff Buff Means. What is your name?"

The man said, "I'm John Horning."

Buff asks the man if he had chest pains. The man said, "It feels like an elephant is sitting on my chest."

Buff said, "Help is on the way." The man flatlined. He didn't have a pulse.

He asked a ranger, "Blow two deep breaths in the man's mouth after I do 30 chest compressions."

A minute later two paramedics came over the ladder and one of the paramedics told Buff, "You don't have to give breaths."

"Don't tell me how to do CPR," Buff said. "Get your asses over here and shock him!" The paramedics moved swiftly. They put the man on 15 liters of oxygen with a mask. The paramedics put the paddles on his chest and shocked him and they soon had a heart rhythm.

One paramedic took Buff to the side and she said, "Look at this strip. Here's what we call a gravestone rhythm."

Buff said, "Well, that doesn't sound good."

Buff said, "Let's get Search and Rescue to get this guy in an ambulance and get him to the hospital as fast as we can."

They tied a rope to the front of the backboard. Two Search and Rescue men lowered their

victim to the ground. A paramedic said to Buff, "You've got a man who seems to trust you; so stay with him holding the rope on the back of the rolling stretcher; so it doesn't get away from the rescuers."

At first they had to carry him over a huge boulder field and then they reached the ground where they wheeled him down to the ambulance.

The man lived nine more years and everybody was surprised. Buff met John once for coffee and he looked well. John said, "Thanks for saving my life."

Buff said, "I had lots of help."

John said, "You and the ranger did the CPR; so I figured you saved my life."

Buff said, "I was just doing my job."

Buff was driving around just listening to the radio. A dispatcher said, "We've got a brush and timber fire 15 miles southwest of Rockerville. If anyone can help please get up there."

Buff got to the fire and talked to Chief Smith who said, "The fire has traveled 45 miles in just an hour. It is incredibly windy. We can't get any of our large fire trucks down that narrow winding road. We already have two brush trucks down there."

When Buff got to the bottom of the narrow very curvy road, he saw the two brush trucks heading for him. A brush truck driver was Mike George. He said that the road has fire on both sides.

Luckily a fire burns downhill much slower than up. Buff drove up to where there was a fire on both sides of the road. Now he had a choice to make. Turn around and watch probably a large number of people die of fire or smoke inhalation or continue down the road. He continued down the road. He finally got past where the fire hadn't gotten yet. He saw people standing in the road. He drove up to the first two and said, "Get in the back and make yourself small."

He next reached a woman with two small children. He told them to get in the back of his Bronco and make themselves small. He then reached three women standing in the road and he told them to get in the back of his Bronco. He found six more people and had them pack in. Now his Bronco was full and he started back to where the fires were burning on both sides of the road. The fire got here fast, he thought.

Buff thought they weren't going to get out because of all the burning trees on each side of the road. The paint was peeling off the Bronco. For a minute, he couldn't see anything but flames. Suddenly they heard an airplane. They hoped it was coming to help them. All of a sudden the Bronco was hit hard by a slurry drop from the airplane. They could see ahead of them now.

Buff quickly drove out and they got transportation for Buff's lucky passengers. He then went and searched for someone else he could help. The fire burned a record 83,000 acres and 200 homes. The droughts seem to be getting worse. We now have fires nearly year-round, Buff thought.

Buff called Randy Moore and told him that Lucky was ten years old and he wanted to have another dog to take his place for the hard work. "Is it too soon to get another dog now?" he asked.

Randy said, "No, not at all! As it happens, I have a Malinois for $110,000 that is fully trained and will be as good as Lucky is."

"I'll send you the money, and you send me the dog." Buff was grinning from ear to ear.

Randy said, "I think you'll love this dog."

"I'm sure I will if you say so," Buff said.

The dog arrived at Buff's home in only two days.

Buff called Randy to thank him.

Randy said, "I hope you'll call him Giant because he weighs 87 pounds."

"I'll do it," Buff said.

Buff decided to build a 10' wall for the dogs to try to climb. When the new dog got there, he told Lucky to climb the wall. Lucky got his paws over the top of the ledge easily. Giant climbed the wall too. Buff thought I was right, Lucky could climb a ten-foot wall.

He trained the dogs to walk across the twenty-five-foot gap using only two ropes strung across. Giant had watched Lucky do it, and in a couple of days, he could do it just as well. Buff taught Giant the Back flip and the Hug. He decided that the Belgian Malinois had to be one of the smartest dog breeds in the world. They were certainly the most tireless, and active dogs in the world.

Buff was searching for an 11-year-old boy in Florida. He and Giant had flown there quickly as they could when they were called.

He took Giant because Lucky had cancer surgery. He seemed to be doing alright, but he knew Giant had much more stamina than Lucky would after having surgery, and he had no idea how far they had to walk.

Buff walked about eight miles with Giant when he found the boy sitting on a log, crying. The boy's dog was by his side, and Giant, trained to stay alert, didn't greet the other dog until Buff motioned with a hand signal that it was okay. Upset, the boy said urgently, "I'm sorry - I just kept following my dog and got lost."

Buff called for a truck to pick up the boy and his dog on a road about a mile away. The boy seemed strong. The truck took him to the hospital to get him checked out just in case. Buff returned to Rapid City.

A year later, Buff saw on the news that hurricane Maxine was heading straight for eastern Florida's coast.

Another big hurricane formed in the Gulf of Mexico named Karen. The two hurricanes merged at the bottom of Florida. The two hurricanes had merged into one and now had winds of 185 miles per hour and a storm surge of 28 feet.

The mayor of Miami, Mayor Samuelson called Buff on the phone, and asked Buff, "When can you get here?" Buff told him he'd be in the air in a couple of hours.

Samuelson said, "I'll meet you at the airport."

Buff got his best friend, Mike, his neighbor to watch Lucky, but Buff said, "Don't push his workouts too hard, because he's still recovering from surgery."

When Buff landed at the Miami airport, he was met by the Mayor and shown to a hangar to keep his airplane.

The mayor said, "Currently we have winds of 140 MPH and it is expected to greatly intensify. It's heading straight for Miami and most of the landfall predictions point to Miami."

Buff learned the Miami airport was only nine feet above sea level. It looked likely that the airport would be inundated. Buff thought to himself, "Well, I guess there goes my airplane."

Buff told Mayor Samuelson, C-130s could land with water and supplies at the airport. The runway only had a small amount of damage so far.

Buff called the Governor and asked him to get scores of chainsaws and more axes and at least 200 boats.

The storm would eventually hit New York as a category-two hurricane. Buff, the mayor, and many heads of rescue and disaster services met in a shelter building thirty miles from the coast. The mayor first asked if anyone had any ideas, and of course, Buff was the only one to stand forward.

"This will be one of the worst natural disasters in American history. We need rescue helicopters, we need places to house those rescued and one place for the cadavers."

"As soon as the winds subside to 50 miles per hour, we should start Search and Rescue," Buff said.

"It looks like Maxine is going to head up I 95 and Inundate areas from Miami Beach, Miami, Hallandale, Hollywood, Dania Beach, Pompano Beach, Deerfield Beach, Boca Raton,

Delray Beach, Lake Worth, Palm Beach, West Palm Beach, North Palm Beach, Juno Beach, and Jupiter. It will continue up the east coast as a weakened storm to New York City. Have the mayor call the army and the National Guard and tell them we need all the help they can give. Tell them that this storm is likely to be the most devastating storm they've ever seen. Call all the states and ask for help to restore power. Ask them to bring trained Search and Rescue Malinois or German Shepherds. We need all we can get," Buff said.

The Army, Coast Guard, and hundreds of people who had boats of all kinds including wind boats, soon were staged thirty miles inland waiting for the winds to drop below 50 MPH.

Hurricane Karen roared out of the Gulf of Mexico as a category 4 storm. It merged with the category 5 Maxine and made a monstrous storm. When the combined hurricane Maxine hit Miami, it destroyed all the stick-built homes. It traveled thirty miles inland in some places. Thousands of people who didn't evacuate were drowned or killed in other ways.

They had to wait for hours for the winds to get down to or below 50 MPH. They all got busy at the site of the worst devastation. They saw that all of the special glass on the east side of the buildings were blown out.

Buff had carried five pairs of protective dog boots on the airplane. Buff put the first pair on Giant along with his bulletproof vest for protection from debris during his search.

"Get into areas that have water up to the roof lines," he asked the volunteers. "I need 25 boats, six boats filled with rescuers, and 19 boats waiting for survivors or cadavers. We also need more chainsaws."

He asked to speak to someone who knows the most about Florida's topography. The man, Jeff Wilson, was brought to him and told Buff about the southern coast's topography. Buff asked the man to join him in a survey to find the area where they could be of most benefit. They jumped into the helicopter and flew over the flooded sites.

Most of southern Florida had thirty inches of rain so flooding was rampant. The helicopter traveled eighteen miles inland and Jeff said look, these homes have water up to the roof. They made arrangements to meet at the site. Soon, Buff had his boats and rescuers ready with axes, chainsaws, and pry bars. Buff had his boat pull up to the nearest house. He told Giant to search. Giant alerted on the roof. Buff yelled out to the people in the attic and they quickly cut a large hole to pull the trapped people out. First, they handed out two infants, which rescuers placed in the boat, next came an elderly woman. Buff leaned in and grabbed her by the black of her blouse and pulled her out with one hand. The elderly woman joined the infants in the boat.

Next came a young woman and a young man who were taken to the boat. Buff asked if anyone else was in there. They shook their heads no. Buff moved on to the next roof as other Search and Rescuers were cutting holes in roofs as they went down the line. Buff cut a hole in the next roof after Giant alerted. He yelled, "How many people are in there?"

A man answered, "There are nine of us." Buff and other rescuers pulled them out of the attic and put them in a large boat. He told the boat owner where they were lodging the rescued and sent him on his way.

Buff had a radio and he asked for more boats and rescue chainsaws. He asked if he could get boats with lights to continue the search into the night.

They said they'd be on the way with lights. They worked through the night as the water started to recede. They had rescued over four hundred and fifty people and now they could send in wind boats and other boats to rescue those on the second floors.

They moved to another flooded neighborhood. Soon there were more rescue boats all over the area. Buff asked the governor to move some of the rescuers up to Miami Beach, Hillandale, Hollywood, Dana Beach, Pompano Beach, Deerfield Beach, and Boca Raton.

Maxine was crawling along at seven miles an hour up the coast and was not losing any wind speed.

The storm surge had retreated, and Buff took a team closer to the coast. Homes built to withstand category five storms were all damaged. Some were blown off their foundations. Businesses were leveled except for a few concrete structures. Buff, Giant and his crew searched the previously inundated coast buildings. All they were finding now were dead bodies. Giant could go up to a house and alert if anyone was alive or if there were any cadavers in the house. There was no one alive.

Maxine damaged Miami Beach tremendously. Hallandale was flooded and flattened. There were now Search and Rescue people coming from almost every state. Day after day, Buff and Giant worked up the coast. He estimated seventy thousand people died in Miami alone. It would take a week to find out the death toll up the coast. The estimate was a hundred and forty thousand people were killed.

By the fifth day, they had a hundred and fifteen thousand cadavers. The president declared a national emergency and sent in the army coast guard and National Guard. Extensive damage was caused from Miami to New York City.

It flooded the New York City subway and other places. Giant had found hundreds of cadavers; they had to get another building for cadavers because they had filled the other one.

Seven days after Maxine hit Miami, Miami Beach, and other towns up the coast, Maxine sped up to fifteen MPH on the ground and headed for New York.

Buff told Governor Bailey he had to go home and check on his dog, Lucky, who was recovering from cancer surgery.

When Buff got home with Giant he went into the house and Lucky limped up to him. Lucky was in great pain. The next day Buff took Lucky to the vet. He was told the chemo didn't work and Lucky only had a day or two left. He took him home and gave him all the love he could.

The next night at two in the morning, he went to check on Lucky who was lying by the refrigerator. He touched Lucky and Lucky cried out. He called the vet and asked him to come over and put him to sleep. He told the vet, even with the slightest touch, Lucky whined and flinched.

The vet came over and prepared a syringe. He found the vein, slipped the needle in, and pushed the plunger. Immediately, Lucky relaxed and he was at peace.

Buff picked Lucky up and held him in his arms and he started crying. The vet asked gently, "Do you want to cremate him?"

And Buff said, "No. I'll bury him on the back of my property tomorrow."

The next day, Buff pulled out his best tablecloth and wrapped Lucky in it. He took Lucky behind the obstacle course and lay him down. He got a shovel and dug a five-foot-deep hole. He lowered Lucky into the grave, filled it in, and patted it down. As soon as he had tamped down the dirt, he collapsed and started wailing. He wept for ten minutes before he got up and went back to the house, feeling like he'd lost his best friend. Giant met him. Buff said Hug and Giant jumped into his arms. He thought, "Thank God I have Giant." Buff already loved Giant almost as much as he loved Lucky. Buff wished that dogs lived longer than 12 to 15 years.

Buff and Giant went to search for an eight-year-old girl missing from the Rockerville Children's Center. He let Giant sniff the girl's unwashed clothes and went on the search. Giant led him on a five-mile walk through the woods where they found her on the bank of a creek. He checked her out and she seemed fine. He carried her on his back to the house. The staff almost hugged him to death. They loved up Giant too for fifteen minutes. Buff felt better than he had in a long time.

Buff got a call from the sheriff who told him they had a large meth operation halfway to Pine Ridge Reservation. Buff asked, "Can I get Giant close enough to the building to sniff?"

The sheriff said, "Sure, all the windows have been blacked out."

That night, the sheriff, Buff, and six other law enforcement officers surrounded the building. The sheriff said, "We don't think they are dangerous - just a couple of guys making money."

Buff led Giant up to the large concrete building by a door. He sniffed the bottom of the door and alerted. There were drugs inside. The sheriff had a search warrant in his hand in twenty minutes. "I'll take the back door with Murphy," Buff said. The others took places 25 feet from the door.

Buff heard the sheriff call with his bullhorn, "Come out! You are surrounded. There is no way out. Come out with your hands on your heads." Buff and Murphy pulled their guns at the back door.

The back door shattered and three people came running out with AR-15s in their hands. They started to aim at Buff and Murphy.

Buff's 44 magnum, boomed twice and hit two of the men in the heart. Murphy shot the other man in the stomach and he dropped to the ground.

Buff went up to the gut-shot man and saw he was gasping and he'd probably suffered a ruptured artery. Two minutes later he was dead.

Buff and Murph went into the meth lab and were astonished at what they found. There must have been five hundred pounds of Opioids. Seven hundred pounds of meth, four hundred pounds of marijuana, and a hundred pounds of fentanyl. They called the governor and the medical examiner, and for more backup. The medical examiner said, "It looks like a good shooting. Let me check their pockets." The medical examiner found billfolds on all three of them, and back at the station, they checked out the info. They took prints and found they were all ex-cons and belonged to the gang called the Bandits.

Federal Marshalls got a search warrant and seized the Bandits' warehouse. They confiscated twenty-two AR-15s and another hundred pounds of meth, 400 pounds of marijuana, and 50 pounds of fentanyl. Some of the pills were made to look like candy; so the youngsters would ingest them.

For the next two years, Buff and Giant found a few cadavers in a lake. He found someone's lost dog, he went to multiple "one thousand" year floods.

On August 7, a F5 tornado hit Oklahoma City. It had wind speeds of 285 miles per hour. It was a mile wide and it touched down 20 miles from the city. It leveled 75 farms, many buildings, and killed hundreds of cattle.

The storm stayed on the ground for 205 miles. It had a diameter of 2.6 miles and plowed through Oklahoma city leveling everything in its path. The downtown high rises had their siding torn off and windows were broken. Buff called the mayor and told him, he was Buff Means and he had a tremendous Search and Rescue dog.

Mayor York said, "I know of you. Please get here as soon as you can."

Buff said, "I can fly down in my newly bought, used 2013 Beechcraft and be there in four and a half hours."

When he got to the airport he was met by Mayor York. The mayor said, "You've been to many disasters with your dog. Please help us figure out what to do."

"Can you get a helicopter to inspect the damage?" Buff asked.

In ten minutes they were in a chopper flying over the damaged city. Buff told the mayor he would like to start in the neighborhood where all the houses were leveled; he was standing in a rubble field. He put on Giant's nail-proof boots and told him to search. Giant alerted to a leveled house with a basement.

Buff yelled, "Is anyone down there?"

A loud voice yelled back that there were seven of them. Volunteers started showing up in great numbers. He and three other rescuers cleared the staircase of debris to the basement. Seven uninjured men, women, and children walked out of the basement.

One of the rescued asked if Buff would search all the leveled houses in the neighborhood. She said, "I have many good friends here."

Smiling gently, Buff said, "That's what we're here for."

Giant alerted at the next house that also had a basement. Buff yelled, "Is anyone down there?"

A man's voice came back, "Yes, there are twelve of us."

Buff and a couple of others cleared the staircase and the people came out. He called the mayor, and said, "We're gonna need as many ATVs and four-wheel drives as possible. We're going to need all the construction equipment like bulldozers and backhoes on-site immediately."

While he spoke, Buff watched hundreds of people wandering around in the street and leveled buildings. Many were in shock.

Many of the people nearby asked if they could help. Buff said, "Go south of here and start looking for cadavers and survivors."

It took five days for enough construction equipment to clear most of the roads. They set up a shelter in the civic center with room for thousands of survivors.

Seven more handlers with Search and Rescue dogs showed up. Together they were clearing as many as 28 of the demolished homes an hour. All parts of the path of destruction were now being searched. Buff left for home after eight days.

He learned that 450 people were killed and 2,015 people injured. It was the most destructive tornado in history. Buff thought to himself, why doesn't everybody believe in climate change? Hurricanes, tornadoes, floods, droughts, and forest fires have already become more severe.

On a sunny warm fall day, the temperature was 72 degrees Fahrenheit. Buff was walking down Main Street. They had so many fine stores to window shop. He heard a loud crash and then another and saw a big black truck barreling down the parking meters knocking them over. They were heading straight for Buff and he jumped into an alcove that was six feet from the door. Buff had pulled his 44 magnum and he decided to take a risk. He shot the rear tire with his 44 magnum and it exploded. Buff didn't dare to shoot again because of the other pedestrians and cars in his way.

He heard several sirens. Buff ran back to his Bronco and started to chase the black truck. The back tire of the truck had ripped off and he couldn't make very good time. Buff took a left on Kansas City street and he saw four patrol cars blocking the road ahead. Eight officers were behind their cars with their guns pointed at the truck. Buff walked up to the back of the truck and yelled, "Get out of the truck with your hands on your heads."

They complied. When they were searched they both had Glock pistols. "Good to see you guys again. An attempted murder charge should also keep you guys locked up for a long time. Why are the Bandits trying to kill me anyway?" Buff asked.

One of the Bandits said, "You gotta go. You killed two of our guys and now it's payback time."

Buff said, "No, you're going to spend 20 years in lock up, and we can handle your buddies." Two police officers took the two Bandits to jail. Buff called the sheriff and told him what had happened.

Buff said, "I think they'll come tonight so could you have some backup for me all night?"

The sheriff said, "Absolutely. I'll send 10 Deputies to hide around your home right now."

"It will soon get dark so we better get moving." Buff got home and took out two AR-15s and a Glock. He kept his 44 magnum on his side. It soon was pitch black and Buff waited until some of the deputy Sheriffs saw two black trucks back into the cover of the trees about 200 yards from Buff's place. Five guys got out of each truck and headed for the big house. They all had AR-15s and 357 magnums.

Two guys stood at the front door ready to kick it in when the two guys at the back door were ready to do the same.

One of the deputies said drop your weapons and put your hands on your heads. The 10 Bandits started firing wildly at the 10 deputies and Buff and the other officers shot them all dead. Buff asked a Deputy, "Will you call the coroner, and the medical examiner, and get some guys in trucks to help carry the bodies?"

The deputy said, "I'm on it." It took hours to finish working the scene of the crime. Then Buff finally got to go to bed.

Roughly twenty years before, even before he went in the Marines, Buff took a composition class. During his study for that class, he heard of climate change. It interested him; so he decided to research it and use it as the subject for his final essay.

The research he did to learn more about climate change, also led him to learn more about Overpopulation, The Sixth Great Extinction Event, and Plastic in our oceans.

After composition class was over, Buff continued his research and began writing letters to editors of large papers. As time went on, he wrote a book called *Our One Chance* and a screenplay about these extreme problems.

All his life, Buff kept reading about and actually seeing firsthand all the evidence of climate change and the other man-made problems the earth was facing. The incredible storms and fires faced by humans really opened his eyes. He decided to try to get on all the major news channels which wouldn't be too hard to do because he was very famous through all the rescues he, Giant, and Lucky led.

He planned to start by giving a speech at a local high school on these subjects to practice his speaking skills before going on TV.

Buff made an appointment to talk to the Rapid City High School Principal, Mark Nielsen. Mark had bright red hair and very pale freckled skin. He was so Irish it could have been written on his forehead. Mark dressed casual-business and spoke in a very relaxed manner. He'd practiced patience a lot since he was the principal of a high school for many years.

Buff took his book and screenplay with him to the meeting. The principal stood up and went to the door when Buff knocked.

The men shook hands and made introductions. The principal looked slowly upward until he found Buff's face. He smiled broadly and sat back down at his desk. Buff took a seat on the other side.

"It is so good to meet you, Buff. Can I call you Buff?"

"Of course," Buff answered.

"Well, Buff, I have followed your and Lucky and Giant's accomplishments since you first became a deputy."

"Thank you very much. I was just trying to help as many people as I could," Buff stated.

Buff handed Mr. Nielsen copies of his book, an article written about him by the Rapid City Journal, and his screenplay. As he handed them over, Mr. Nielsen looked each one over.

"Have you read them?" Buff asked.

"I've read your many letters to the editor and I'm very interested in reading your book and screenplay."

"Thank you. Let me know what you think. I would like to address the seniors; so they could know the true state of the world."

"You are most welcome to give a speech to the senior class. Let's set the date for October 11th, if it works for you?"

"It does, and thank you, Mr. Nielsen," Buff grinned and shook hands with the principal.

When the time came, Buff took the stage in the school's theater which could seat 1,500 students. They only had 900 seniors so the principal had asked 600 juniors to attend too. When Buff was introduced, they gave him a standing ovation.

Buff greeted the students by saying, "Metakuye Oyiasin - which means, 'All my relatives' in the language of the Lakota Sioux. I am here to try and show you that we, the human race on this planet, have reached the tipping point.

"Students, what I'm going to tell you today is not pleasant, but it is necessary. We know it will be hard, out of our normal routines, and expensive, but we have NO CHOICE in this if we want to save our planet. Every place on earth must change to renewable energy now.

"Climate Change is the greatest threat to the human race. We've already raised the world's temperature by 1.1° Celsius. We are seeing more and larger wildfires, more and worse flooding, and stronger and more destructive typhoons and hurricanes. We are having more severe and longer droughts, widespread crop failures, more frequent heat waves, and dramatic shifts in plant and animal ranges."

Buff quoted the Intergovernmental Panel on Climate Change, the I.P.C.C., "Global Warming is dangerously close to spiraling out of control."

"The world is already certain to face further climate disruptions for decades if not for centuries to come. Human activities are unequivocally to blame for climate change. An I.P.C.C. report said, and I quote, 'The

UN secretary-general, Antonio Gutierrez, describes the report as a CODE RED for humanity.' The alarm bells are deafening,'" Buff said.

"This report should sound the death knell for coal and fossil fuels before they destroy our planet. The world's most vulnerable are those with the fewest resources and will suffer the most.

"In the journal, Nature, they said that in just 18.5 years we will have packed enough co2 in the atmosphere to cause an increase of a 2° Celsius rise at the very minimum. This will cause climate change to become much more disastrous. Several studies have shown that a 4° centigrade rise in temperature could be reached by 2100. It is inevitable if we don't turn to green energy now.

"Since 1958, measurements have shown that the Arctic Ocean ice cover has lost more than two-thirds of its thickness as averaged across the arctic at the end of the summer. Older ice has shrunk by almost 18,000 square miles.

"If we do nothing, the world will continue to warm much faster than if it stayed in the habitable range. If we wait any longer, a great deal of Greenland's Ice Sheet will continue to melt quickly, raising the ocean water levels by at least 10 inches.

"Antarctica's Thwaites Ice Shelf could shatter within five years. It would raise sea levels by 3-10 feet. The demise of the ice shelf could also destabilize west Antarctica which locks away around 16 feet of sea level rise. With a sea level rise of several meters total, many of the world's major cities, including Shanghai, New York, Miami, Tokyo, and Mumbai will flood swathes of land in coastal regions. Low-lying nations like Kiribati, Taiwan, and the Maldives will be underwater.

"If we get a 3-foot sea level rise it will adversely affect 400 million people. Even if we significantly curb emissions in the coming decades, more than a third of the world's remaining glaciers will melt before the year 2100.

"When it comes to sea ice, 95% of the oldest and thickest ice in the Arctic is already gone. In a couple of decades when the Arctic Ocean is ice-free in the summers, the dark, exposed water will soak up the heat, further warming our planet.

"Ask the city to put solar panels on all our city and governmental buildings. They will pay for themselves. Get your rich friends to make commercials that tell us how fast we have to change. We are at the edge of reaching several tipping points. Every one of us is responsible for the state of the earth. If you don't take any action, and I mean every one of you, in 2050 you'll be saying why didn't I do more to help keep the planet habitable for future generations? Thank you all for listening."

Buff shook hands with the principal and left the stage while the students were still applauding.

Buff went on the campaign trail for Bailey. He went to all fifty states with Giant. He found he was a great public speaker. During each speech, he had Giant 'Hug,' 'Flip,' and 'Stand' to walk on his hind legs. The crowds went wild. God, everybody loved that dog.

The presidential election was a landslide for Governor Bailey. He gave a wonderful inaugural speech. Buff went on the road telling people how much President Bailey's policies would help them. His vice president was Daria Nickerson.

"Good afternoon," President Bailey said.

Most of the crowd replied, "Good Afternoon!"

His speech was well received and everyone knew they had done a good thing when they voted for him.

Chief Sheriff's Deputy Buff Means stood at the podium with President Bailey in the Rose Garden. There were 1,000 people in attendance. There were scores of networks covering the event. ABC, CBS, FOX, and NBC were all there along with media from ¾ of the countries of the world.

Buff, by this time, was known to the world. He knew his speech and the speeches of his experts must affect the majority of people in the U.S. and around the world. Otherwise, we would experience a hellish nightmare in the future.

Chief Deputy Sheriff Means said, "Now, I'd like to ask every one of you to do your part in mitigating climate change, overpopulation, the Sixth Great Extinction Event, and plastic in our ocean."

"I have with me Dr. John Thompson from Hanover, a world-renowned expert on Climate Change."

"We also have, Dr. Gene Steineker from Oxford. He is considered the most knowledgeable man in the world on the Sixth Great Extinction Event.

"Also, Professor Mann of the University of California will explain why we are in so much trouble with plastic and the warming of our oceans.

"Dr. Craig Jones from Berkeley is here, and he is the most knowledgeable man on Overpopulation.

"So first, let me introduce Dr. John Thompson to speak to you about Climate Change," Buff said loudly.

Dr. Thompson went to the podium and said, "Thank you for inviting me to speak here. Climate Change is the worst problem that the world faces today. Buff was right, we are heading for the collapse of civilization within 2 to 3 decades unless we greatly decrease our use of fossil fuels. Emissions, at our present rate, will make us pass our benchmark of a 1.5° C rise in temperatures. At our current rate of inaction, we are going to quickly raise our temperatures by more than most climate experts believe.

"Our planet's average temperature could see as much as a 9.7° F or 5.4° C rise by 2100. A rise like that would make much of the world uninhabitable. It is an existential thing, but we can do something about it. We need to spend billions of dollars on solar arrays and wind power. All government buildings should solar panels on them within 1-2 years.

"The Arctic is already warming at more than twice the rate as the rest of the globe. It is a phenomenon known as Arctic amplification. Almost all climate researchers agree that this is human-caused climate change. The Arctic permafrost is rapidly melting and causing the release of massive amounts of CO2 and methane gas. Methane is up to 80 times more potent than CO2 as a greenhouse gas.

"The tundra of the Western Arctic Circle had been carpeted in blueberries, cranberries, cloudberries, shrubs, and lichens that have provided abundant food for grizzly bears, caribou, and many other animals. However, as permafrost and the slumping of the ground expands, great parts of the landscape are being transformed into nothing but mud silt and melted peat moss which is releasing massive amounts of carbon that has been stored in the permafrost for millennia. The Arctic has lost 228 gigatons of ice per year over the past decade.

"In Alaska, average temperatures have increased by 4.7° F since 1970.

"In 2019, scientists found evidence that warm water was indeed flowing under the base of the glaciers in Antarctica, melting them from underneath.

"The doomsday glacier or the Thwaites glacier could raise sea levels by 16 feet after it melts. Scientists say the glacier is nearly the size of Florida. The loss of the Thwaites glacier could decimate West Antarctica.

"If the West Antarctic ice sheet collapses, the most widely cited estimate of global mean sea level rise would result in a 16 foot rise in sea level overall. More than half the population of Florida towns and cities live on land below a four foot level.

"NASA analysis shows that the year 2020 was the hottest year on record. The 8 hottest years have all happened in the last eight years. 2022 was the 5th hottest year on record.

"Scientific records have been kept since 1880, and it is no coincidence that all these eight hottest years have happened in the last 8 years. That the conditions are changing so fast, is further proof that human beings are causing climate change.

"Since 1960, atmospheric levels of all CO2 have increased dramatically. In 1880, CO2 levels were 291 parts per million. Today CO2 levels are 441 parts per million. It looks like we are going to pass the 2° Centigrade rise for sure, making parts of the planet uninhabitable unless we act now. CO2 levels are higher now than millions of years ago.

"I was asked to keep this short; so I'll leave you with this. If you don't 'believe' climate change is real, you are ignorant. Not ignorant about everything, but ignorant about climate change. Research it for a couple of hours. When I say we must act now, I mean NOW!!!"

Buff returned to the podium as Dr. Thompson walked away. "Thank you Dr. John Thompson. We appreciate your being here."

Buff continued, "Now I introduce you to Dr. Gene Steineker, the most knowledgeable man on the Sixth Great Extinction Event."

There was loud applause. A very tall, skinny man with a beard, Dr. Steineker began by asking those in the crowd how many of them knew of the Sixth Great Extinction Event. Only a few hands went up.

Steineker said, "The Sixth Great Extinction Event shows how 8 billion people are ruining the environment. The Sixth Great Extinction Event is almost exclusively driven by human impact. Thirty percent to fifty percent of all species will likely have gone extinct by 2050 unless we act now.

"Can you imagine a planet without tigers, elephants, rhinos and so many more species? We are guilty of not being good stewards of God's creation. We are taking over the habitats that animals rely on. Among these is interconnectedness between humans and all animals. One species going extinct could cause the extinction of many more animals. Every 20 minutes an animal or plant goes extinct.

"Some of the animals that are likely to go extinct by 2050, unless we change our ways, are lions, elephants, pandas, pangolins, sea turtles, bees, polar bears. Of course many more animals will go extinct. It's truly staggering how many animal species are currently critically endangered.

"The rhinoceros, emperor penguins, Borneo orangutans, Amur leopards, and Sumatran elephants are just a fraction of the species that will go extinct by 2100.

"At the minimum, 558 of our large species could go extinct by 2100 and millions of small animals will go extinct with them.

"We have to get together all over the world to mitigate climate change, the Sixth Great Extinction Event, overpopulation, and plastic in our ocean.

"The Holocene Extinction, which we are going through, is now known as the Sixth Great Extinction event. The Ordovician and Celeron extinction events, and the late Devonian extinction, the Permian Triassic Extinction event and the Cretaceous Paleocene Extinction event are the other past Extinction events. Mass extinction events are characterized by the loss of at least 75% of species within a geographically short time.

"In *The Future of Life*, 2020, Edward Osborne Wilson of Hanover calculated that if the current rate of human destruction of the biosphere continues more than one-half of every species will be extinct by 2100.

"The historical typical extinction rate in terms of the natural evolution of the planet and the current rate of extinction is 10 to a thousand times higher than in any of the previous mass extinctions in the history of the earth.

"There is widespread consensus among scientists that human activity is accelerating the extinction of many animal species through the destruction of their habitats, the consumption of animals as resources, and the elimination of species that humans view as threats or competitors. The fact is that humans have become the primary driver of modern extinctions. The undeniable rapidly rising extinction trend impacting numerous animal groups including mammals, birds, reptiles and amphibians has prompted scientists to declare a biodiversity crisis.

"Some scholars assert that the emergence of capitalism as a dominant economic system has accelerated ecological exploitation, destruction and has accelerated mass species extinction."

"Thank you, Dr. Steineker," Buff said. "I'd now like to introduce Dr. Mann, the foremost expert on Plastic in the Ocean."

Dr. Mann came to the podium and said, "Good afternoon. The ocean contains 24.4 trillion pieces of micro plastics. They are the size of a sesame seed. 99% of all seabirds will be eating plastic by 2050.

"Scientists have found cigarette lighters, bottle caps, model cars, and all types of plastic in dead bird's stomachs. By 2050, 99% of all seabirds will have some amount of plastic in them. Research suggests that sea birds will be extinct by 2100, and now probably sooner.

"Let me tell you about the catastrophe of plastic in our ocean. There are now 51 trillion macro and micro pieces of plastic in our ocean. China, Thailand and several other countries are still allowing garbage to be dumped into rivers, streams and creeks that reach the ocean and they dump garbage into the ocean itself.

"Plastic in our ocean will outweigh all the fish in the ocean by 2050. Fish in the North Pacific Ocean consume about 24,000 tons of plastic per year, macro plastics and even smaller bits called nanoplastics can move from a fish's stomach to the muscle tissue, the part that humans eat. Plastic left in the water for a long time releases many toxic chemicals into the water. Nanoplastics damage aquatic creatures as well as birds and likely humans.

"The they eat often blocks their digestive tracts diminishing the need to eat and altering feeding behaviors all of which reduces growth or diminishes productive output. It also causes death.

"In the last decade alone the proportion of fish consuming plastic has risen dramatically in all species. In studies published from 2010 to 2013, we found an average of 20% of the fish sampled contained plastic. In studies published from 2017 to 2019, that share has risen to 33%; so the number of fish containing poisonous plastic is increasing yearly. Thousands of seabirds, sea turtles, seals and other marine animals are killed each year after ingesting plastic or getting entangled in discarded plastic nets or other plastic debris.

"Endangered wildlife like Hawaiian monk seals and Pacific loggerhead sea turtles are among nearly 700 species that eat plastic or get caught in plastic litter."

"Given the trends, more than 99% of seabirds will have ingested plastic by 2050. Seabirds mistake plastic floating in the water for food because it has algae growing on it and it smells like food to them. This causes injury or death to sea birds. The birds feed their chicks plastic, causing the chicks to all die from starvation.

"I've seen many pictures of dead sea birds lying on their backs decomposing, exposing their open bellies full of plastic. They can't digest the plastic or excrete it.

"An estimated 70% of fish populations are overused, overfished, or in crisis as a result of fishing; there will not be enough fish to commercially fish by 2050.

"A total of over 100,000 marine creatures die because they get entangled in plastic debris each year. Thank you very much for listening."

"Now I'd like to introduce you to Dr. Craig Jones," Buff said.

Dr. Craig Jones went to the podium, and said, "I'm going to be telling you why we have a very narrow window to save our planet. Our population has reached the Red Zone. We are crossing the tipping point."

"Overpopulation is the cause of many of our problems in the world today. If you have been paying attention, you know that at present, 8 billion people aren't sustainable on our planet and by 2035 we will have a billion more people. Think of the loss of habitat and resources. A great deal of land will be needed for homes, roads, bridges, airports, hospitals, hotels, restaurants, grocery stores, power plants and many other businesses and many other things that would need to be built for a billion more people.

"The population is expected to reach 9.8 billion people by 2050. Adding another 1.1 billion people would put unimaginable stress on our planet's environment. By 2100, there are projected to be 11.2 billion people.

"Africa is the continent with the greatest population growth. We need to provide birth control for all women on the African continent and other countries that need help if they ask for it.

"Places that want birth control and don't have access to it or the money to pay for it, need the most help. Africa's share of the global population increased by 17% in 2020 increased by 39% in 2021 and is expected to increase by 26% by 2050. They need our help.

"Africa has a population of 1,416,977,910 as of Saturday, November 19, 2022. Their population in the next thirty years is expected to exceed more than 2 billion more babies. By 2050, the continent will be home to at least 25% of the world's population compared to less than 10% in 1950.

"The Social Scientist, Luke Kemp analyzed dozens of civilizations, which he defined as a society with agriculture, multiple cities, military dominance in their geographical regions, and a continuous political structure. The average lifespan of a civilization is close to 340 years.

"Environmental problems have contributed to the collapses of civilizations in the past, but now, for the first time, a global collapse caused by mankind seems likely. Overpopulation, overconsumption by the rich, and poor choices of technologies are major drivers. Dramatic cultural change provides the main hope of averting calamity.

"Thank you for your time. I hope your eyes have been opened to these things," Dr. Jones said. "Here is Buff Means again. Thank you all for coming."

Buff Means took the podium next and began, "We mustn't forget the rainforests. The Amazon rainforest has already lost 22% of its territory. In the first half of this year, deforestation claimed roughly 1,500 square miles. Also you need to understand that Fourteen percent of coral reefs were lost between 2009 and 2018 alone. Without drastic action to limit greenhouse gas emissions, coral reefs will almost certainly be extinct by 2100.

"Healthy coral reefs support commercial and subsistence fisheries as well as jobs and businesses through tourism, and recreation.

"When coral reefs disappear, essential food, shelter, and spawning grounds for fish and other marine organisms will cease to exist and biodiversity will greatly suffer as a consequence.

"Coral reefs are nursing grounds for one million aquatic species. In just twenty years scientists estimate about seventy to ninety percent of all coral reefs will disappear primarily as a result of warming ocean waters, ocean acidity, and pollution.

"According to the U.N., around one billion people closely depend on coral reefs for their food and livelihoods. Their disappearance would be catastrophic, resulting in hundreds of millions of people around the world losing their main source of food and income."

"Coral reef structure buffers shorelines against waves, storms, and floods helping to prevent loss of life, property damage, and erosion. Reefs are among the most biologically diverse and valuable ecosystems on earth. Four thousand species of fish are dependent on coral reefs at some point in the cycle," said Buff. "Coral Reefs are called the rainforests of the sea."

Buff pleaded, "My fellow Americans, I ask you to join me in Oneness. If you believe in one God or one earth, or think life just happened we need your help."

"We must look to the future to care for our countless generations to come. Everybody must play a part!

"I'm asking all of you to do everything in your power to stop the destruction of our planet. Write your congressman, write letters to the editor, write your city council, write your mayors and governors.

"There is little doubt that civilization will collapse in just decades unless we become one with each other, are co-creators with God, and One in our efforts."

President Bailey said, "Thank you for listening to us, please help in every way you can, and finally, thank Buff for arranging the speech." There was widespread applause.

"Surrounded by the secret service, the president turned to walk back to the white house. Buff walked next to the president. A man who was sitting in the front row, was only fifteen feet from the president. He rushed the president, stabbing a secret service agent in his back as he moved. He pulled back his ceramic knife and started to stab the president in the back.

Buff threw his arm between the attacker and the president. He took the ceramic knife right through the middle of his palm while not completely stopping the knife. About two inches of the blade still entered the president's back. The secret service pulled the president to the ground while other officers took the man down.

The secret service rushed the president to the hospital and he had emergency surgery. They sewed up the small hole the blade made. The doctor came in and said, "I'm Doctor Early. Your surgeon and I have good news for you. The wound wasn't too bad."

Buff went to the emergency room on his own and got his hand cared for before he headed home to Rapid City.

Buff was tired of traveling all over the world and he had an idea. He called the sheriff's secretary and asked for an appointment. He went to the sheriff's office and Sheriff Carlyle said, "Come in. I've missed your ugly mug."

Buff went into the sheriff's office and they shook hands. Sheriff Carlyle asked, "What can I do for you, Buff?"

"I know this is entirely irregular, but I want to become the chief Deputy Sheriff again, get a good partner and work the streets," Buff said.

"Will you work for $5.00 a month?"

"Yes, that would be great."

"Of course," Carlyle said. "You've made my day. I've wanted to get rid of my worthless Chief Deputy and now is a perfect time. Do you want a partner?"

"Yes, preferably a woman because they make the best partners in my experience."

Carlyle said, "Come with me and I'll introduce you to your new partner." They walked to a cubicle and tapped on the side. A woman Captain looked up.

"I'd like you to meet your new partner. Chief Deputy Buff Means. Buff, this is Captain Jan Samuelsen and she'll be your partner. She is a third degree black belt in Krav Maga. I thought you'd like that," Carlyle said.

Jan stood and strongly shook Buff's hand. "I think we'll be a good team."

"I want you to go after all types of law breakers. I want the two of you to call me any time for any reason," Sheriff Carlyle said.

Buff lost his breath when he met Jan. She was exquisite. She had a small cute nose, high cheekbones, big brown eyes and the most succulent mouth he had ever seen. Her teeth were perfect and bright white.

They went to work driving around town and watching for criminal activity. They got a call from dispatch about the probable abuse of three young children. "A warrant is waiting for you," dispatch said.

The Davidson's live at 1920 Twilight drive. And a woman was seen savagely beating her middle daughter, age five years old by a passerby.

Buff, Jan and Giant went to the house with the warrant in hand. Jan went to the back door and pulled her Glock. Buff went to the front door and knocked. Nobody answered at first. He pounded on the door until a thirtyish year old woman finally answered.

"What do you want?" she asked.

"You can let us in," Buff answered. "Here is the warrant."

"No, you can't come in," she said and slammed the door shut in Buff's face. He kicked the door open and splitters of wood flew all over the place. A man came downstairs to see what the noise was about

"What the fuck are you doing in my house?" he asked when he saw Buff.

"I want to see your three children now."

"You can't - they all have the flu and can't be seen," the father said.

Buff told the man to go sit in the recliner. He asked Jan, who had come inside, to hold the man at gunpoint while he went upstairs.

He checked the first bedroom he came to and found a five year old emaciated boy. Buff said, "I'm here to protect you. Will you let me look you over?"

The boy said, "I'm Brad, and yes you can look me over if you can get us out of here."

"I'm sure I can get you away from here," Buff said.

Buff went to the boy and saw he had a black eye and a previously broken nose. Buff checked over the boy's body after giving the boy a sheet to cover himself. The boy, Brad, had cigarette burns from his feet to his hands. He was black and blue on his back with the imprints of a belt buckle. Buff called down to Jan and asked her to call for backup and three ambulances.

Buff went to the next bedroom and found a three year old girl. She was tiny from being malnourished. He checked her body and found she was covered with cigarette burns and the same strap and belt buckle bruises. In some places her skin had been laid open during a beating.

The first ambulance showed up and Buff asked them to take Mandy and Brad to the hospital. He canceled the third ambulance. Buff went to the next bedroom and found a seven year old boy huddled in the corner. He was filthy and his hair had dried blood all over it.

Buff looked for the wounds and found about a dozen cuts. It looked to Buff that he had been beaten by his dad's belt buckle. His left arm was crooked. He obviously had his arm broken and nobody bothered to set it to heal. He also found cigarette burns all over his body.

Some backup showed up. The two deputy sheriff's cuffed the parents and took them to jail. The other ambulance came and took Nick to the hospital.

Jan had also seen the children's conditions. she said, "I believe I'd like to put 9mm rounds in each of their heads."

The parents, Cal and Lee Davidson, were put into an interrogation room. Jan started asking the questions.

"Why do you beat your children?"

Cal said, "They are like wild animals. We had to control them."

Jan asked Lee, "Why do you beat your children?"

"They are very bad children and that is the only way we can control them."

Jan continued, "You're both under arrest for child abuse, cruelty, endangerment and child neglect. We have your confessions on tape and I hope you spend many decades in prison. I hear that the other prisoners don't like child abusers. You'll probably have to be in solitary confinement for your terms."

"I've never seen such awful child abuse in my life. I hope you enjoy solitude," Buff said.

At the hospital, Nick, the oldest child was taken to surgery to straighten his broken arm. They were all put on special diets with supplements. After about a week the children started to feel safe and started talking to Jan and Buff.

It looks like they have made a full physical recovery, but a mental recovery could take years for the five and seven year old boys.

Social services were called in to evaluate the children and to find a place where all three could live together. The social workers found them to be three of the sweetest kids they'd ever met. They took Mandy, Brad and Nick to the Fisher's house. The Fisher's already had one eight year old abused boy that they had adopted. Social services had rated them as the best of all the foster parents to take care of these newest victims.

Once the three children had been there a couple of months they started acting like normal children. They started Nick in the first grade because he could read a little bit and was a very fast learner. The next year they put him in third grade because he had progressed so rapidly.

The Davidsons were eventually given 30 years in prison. Buff and Jan wanted them to spend more time, but 30 years was pretty good.

A few weeks later they were driving down First Street and dispatch called over the radio. A female voice said, "There is an armed robbery at the Sixth Street Casino. There are two men, one is armed with an AR-15 with a Bump stock. He riddled the casino in bullets.

In three minutes Buff and Jan arrived at the scene. They pulled their AR-15s out of the trunk along with body armor. They also had their pistols.

Buff told Jan to go to the back door and find some cover, like behind a dumpster, in case the guy with the automatic rifle comes out of the back door. Buff couldn't help but think, "She's got the finest body shape I've ever seen. She looks like she spends hours working out every day."

Jan couldn't find a dumpster; so she went up to the side door and stood to the side of it. The man with the Bump stock ran out the back door and Jan gave him a sidekick square on the nose. She could hear the bones crushing and he fell over, out cold.

The second gunman was right behind the guy with the Bump Stock and he tripped over his unconscious friend. Jan kicked his gun out of his hand and then jumped on his back.

"Hold still and I won't shoot you!" Jan yelled.

The guy put his hands behind his back and she cuffed him. She then cuffed the other man. Buff came running out of the back door and saw Jan standing there over the two cuffed men. Buff said, "Jan, I hope I never run into you in a dark alley."

"Let's get these scumbags to jail," Jan said.

After the two men were locked up, Buff and Jan went to write their reports. Buff said to Jan, "I hope this doesn't ruin our relationship, but I've never wanted a woman more than you in my life."

"Buff Means, I've never wanted a man more than I want you," Jan said. "I'd like us to be married."

Buff's jaw dropped and he asked, "When?"

She said, "I think tomorrow will be great."

Buff called his friend, Reverend Cleveland and asked him if he could marry them tomorrow afternoon.

He asked, "How does three o'clock tomorrow at my house sound?"

"Perfect," Buff agreed.

Buff and Jan and two friends each got to Reverend Cleveland's house at five minutes before three.

Reverend Cleveland opened the door and said, "Welcome. Who is this beautiful woman?"

Buff said, "This is Jan Samuelsen. Jan, here is your ring." He handed her a two carat ring.

"I just have one question."

"Go ahead, Reverend."

"Jan, how can you marry such a butt - ugly guy like Buff?"

Jan laughed and said, "Well, somebody gotta do it."

"Thanks a lot, both of you!" Buff said. "Let's do this."

Reverend Cleveland performed the marriage ceremony and as tradition dictates ended with, "You may kiss the bride."

Buff and Jan kissed very softly at first, and then they were really making out. After 10 minutes the reverend went to his kitchen and the four guests went outside to wait for them.

Buff thought, "Jan must be the best kisser in the world."

Jan was thinking, "I've never felt so good making out before." They made out for an hour staying in the same spot.

Eventually Jan said, "I imagine I'll move in with you because your place is much bigger."

"That sounds like music to my ears," Buff said.

They went home to Buff's house and went to the bedroom. "I think I'd like a shower," Jan said.

"Me too," Buff said. They got in the shower together and washed each other's bodies slowly and gently. It was bliss for both of them.

They both dried each other off with thick soft towels at the same time. They both loved what they were seeing. Jan slid under the covers and Buff slid in right after her. They started making out. They kissed for an hour. As he entered her, they moved as if they were one. They made love slowly. Every time he was going to cum, Buff stopped until he could start again without cuming. They were in unison for two hours before Buff asked, "Are you ready?"

"More ready than any time in my life!" They came together and they both made incredible vocalizations. The climax was by far the best that either had had in their lives.

Finally Buff rolled off and grabbed Jan's hand. He said, " I love you more than anything."

Jan said, "You took the words right out of my mouth." They slowly started making love again.

Buff thought, "This is what heaven must be like."